Sharman's VINTAGE GARDEN
BY JENNY HASKINS

A quilt and pillows from the Studio of
Jenny and Simon Haskins
along with inspirational projects from friends

RK
RNK DISTRIBUTING

First published in the USA in 2009
By RNK Distributing Inc
Phone: Toll Free 1877 331 0034
Email: info@RNKDistributing.com

Author: Jenny Haskins
Assistant: Simon Haskins
Quilt from the studio of:
Jenny and Simon Haskins
Designer: Jo Martin
Subeditor: Nina Paine
Graphics: Simon Haskins
Photographer: Tom Evangelidis
Styling: Jenny Haskins
Publishing coordinator: Simon Blackall

National Library of Congress
Cataloguing-in-Publication Data applied for

Haskins, Jenny
Haskins, Simon
Sharman's Vintage Garden

ISBN: 978-0-692-00043-4

Printed in China by Toppan Printing

Sharman's VINTAGE GARDEN
BY JENNY HASKINS

*A quilt and pillows from the
Studio of Jenny and Simon
Haskins with inspirational
projects from friends*

From the garden gazebo ...

Sharman's Vintage Garden is a quilt and a book that are all about friendship, flowers and love. Sam, Simon's younger sister and my baby daughter, gave me a book of poems when she was in her early teens. The book, entitled Share Your Love, is by Larry Quick, and Sam's inscription in it reads:

To Mum,
'The more that I share myself, the
more that there is to love.'
I really don't need to say this because
you already know but I love you.
I will always be here for you or if you
need someone to talk to. I hope that
when you read this book and we are
apart it will make you think of me.
Love Sam

SIMON AND I would like to dedicate this book to our many friends who contributed to *Sharman's Vintage Garden* and to our lives, along with family and friends who epitomize the words of the poem by Larry Quick (with some editor's license taken):

You gave us wings and we flew,
You gave us a voice and we sang,
You gave us rhythm and we danced,
You gave us heart and we loved,
You gave us vision and we saw,
You gave us sound and we heard,
You gave us touch and we felt,
You gave us love and we live.

So to our contributors Sharman and Richard Dorsey, Petrina Cude and Angie Wylie (the Sharman's gang), Regula Muller and Bernadette Robinson (the Melann's duo), Laura Haynie, Ricky and Kay Brooks and Debbie Homer (the creative team at RNK Distributing), Margaret Moorehead (our *International Accredited Tutor*) and Maree Mulvaney (whose house we used for styling), you are all as much a part of this book as Simon and I are.

We would be very remiss, however, if we did not mention our 'garden' of family and friends: Poppa, Sam, Laurie, Jason, Kim and baby Cooper, Sue, Kate, Niki and Chris, Cleo, Kirsten and baby Harvey, our family who give us unconditional love. Sue Amour, Robyn Wilson, Lucie Magnay, Sandie Scrivner, Narelle Grieve, Sally Cooper, Gloria McKinnon, Anne Newman, Debbie Ballard, Hans and Roswitha Martini, Jurgen Sanders, Kerrie Hay, Kevin Anderson, Di Hobbes, Jodie Caruana, Kristina Hickey, John Upton, Catherine Heighton, Debi Reece, Sue and Herb Hausmann, Theresa Robinson, Marge Boyle, Barbara Sunderlage, Martha Pullen, Louise Baird, Gail Settle, Ray Smith and Larry Touchette (who although did not directly contribute to this book, are friends of long-standing and have loved and supported us in so many ways).

You are the perfume from our flower beds that we carry with us every day, even if we are not in or near our 'secret garden'.

The *Sharman's Garden* design CD is named in honor of Sharman Dorsey, the essence of love and friendship and a woman who shares her caring unassuming ways with her friends, students, customers and strangers alike. It was she who was the inspiration for the designs on the *Sharman's Garden* design CD.

I first met Sharman at a sewing machine convention back in 1993 and then caught up with her again at the end of an arduous seven-week teaching tour of the US in 1998. Arriving around midnight (with Sharman's being my next-to-last teaching engagement), tired and homesick beyond words, Sharman's warm and loving gang was there to meet me at the airport. My room was filled with flowers and a 'care' basket full of goodies, including a bone china teacup and saucer (as Sharman knew I hated drinking out of a mug!). A male industry colleague once said, 'I can never say no to Sharman'; then there was the Las Vegas bellhop who, after taking her bags out of the car, had chocolate-dipped strawberries delivered to Sharman's room! She is simply irresistible! Richard, her much-loved husband, would totally agree.

So, about the quilt. As purple is my favorite color, Simon reminded me that I was most inspired when I used it, and that our next quilt should therefore be in shades of purple using my personal range of embroidery threads and *Sharman's Garden* embroidery designs. And, as always, Simon had a plan, one he told me about bit by bit. (I think these plans of his are delivered to me in steps, so as not to panic me!) Bear in mind, at the time I was working on our last book, *Jenny's Heritage* – heaven forbid he should put pressure on me!

The larger hooped embroidery machines had been (or were being) released at this time, and Simon said how wonderful it would be for the quilter to be able to embroider one large quilt block in a single hooping. With this in mind, he set about combining the embroidery designs from *Sharman's Garden* in such a way that a 14-inch quilt block could be embroidered in a single hooping – oh joy!

As we didn't have one of these new fangled machines, we called on our friends Margaret, Laura, Regula and

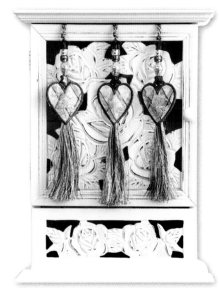

Bernadette (who all did have access to these new wonders) and asked them to embroider the 16 blocks and the center medallion for our quilt. They all agreed, instantaneously – what amazing friends, thank you so much!

So it was thread and fabric-choosing time for me. My new range of embroidery threads was in the throes of manufacture, so my chosen color palette of threads for *Sharman's Vintage Garden* quilt was Express-Posted directly from Japan. There were enough thread sets that we could each have one, thanks to RNK Distributing (who also supplied all the stabilizers and batting for the quilt). Don't forget to glance at the other scrumptious thread combinations (in the second half of the book) that 'our creative gang' has used in their delectable creations, which can be used as possible alternative thread combinations for your version of *Sharman's Vintage Garden*.

Next came the fabric, and this is always hard as whatever I choose seems to be out of production at the time – I choose for color and design rather than availability! It took me some time to find exactly what I had in mind, but when I brought my

chosen fabrics home and laid the threads out on them, the results were just perfect – and so our new quilt was conceived.

From there it was a matter of history repeating itself: once the blocks came back to us the quilt was put together in record time (isn't it always the case). Simon 'fussy-cut' all the sashing, borders and cornerstones (cutting to patterns rather than fabric grain to ensure the perfect matching of patterns), with me stitching the quilt pieces together.

Lizzy Allen, who is a *Jenny Haskins' Accredited Tutor* (as are Bernadette, Margaret, Laura, Debi and Catherine) and the National Demonstrator for Jenny's products in Australia, is also a talented embroiderer and an award-winning long-arm custom quilter. Upon completion, *Sharman's Vintage Garden* quilt was shipped to Lizzy who performed her quilting magic to complete the circle of friendship that is *Sharman's Vintage Garden* quilt.

Laura, Margaret, Melann's, Sharman's and RNK all then contributed amazing projects of their own choosing, design and color, and the results speak for themselves. These are all featured in the second half of this book. So you have an amazing selection of ideas, projects and designs to cultivate in *Sharman's Vintage Garden*. Like a butterfly in a beautiful garden, you can now flit from flower to flower, drinking in the nectar of our embroidered garden of inspirational dreams.

And on that ethereal note, there is nothing more for Simon and I to say except that we wish you dreams that burst into flowers full of love and friendship, as you venture into *Sharman's Vintage Garden*.

Remember – sharing what is there is the ultimate freedom to be all one can be.

Jenny

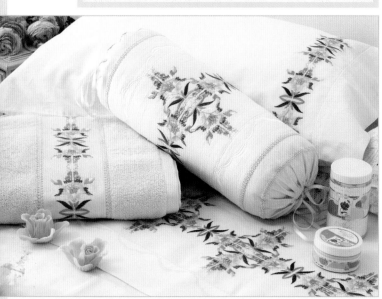

Contents

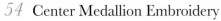

Jenny's garden
of bliss

I delight in the tranquility, joy and sheer bliss of nestling among soft pillows in my cane garden swing as it gently rocks in my Garden of Bliss, a garden which transcends time and the cares of everyday life.

My garden is a sanctuary which has a way of blocking out the world and engulfing me in its sheer splendor. The soothing melody of the gentle tinkle of water accompanied by wind-orchestrated chimes, backed by the hum of the bees and harmonizing twittering of the birds, is carried on a scented breeze, as if swaddling me in a magnificent quilt.

Surely this is what Sharman's Vintage Garden quilt is all about, as it was designed to bring inspiration, self-assurance and happiness into the lives of all who make it. Enjoy the bliss that this book brings; in the words of Ruth Little, 'May it be as a token flower that tells what words can ne'er express so well.'

Is there a fairy at the bottom of my garden?

A Secret Garden conjures up ethereal images along with glorious colors, cottage flowers and rambling roses with their intoxicating perfumes and yes, even fairies somewhere down the back.

AS A FRIEND once said to me, 'Fairies are to me, Jen, what angels are to you.' Do I believe in either? I think both are connected and, like miracles, they happen or appear if you believe in them!

So many stories and poems have been written about fairies and angels in gardens. There is even a fairy or an angel for every flower, and as I relax and unwind at the end of the day in my garden swing, when all is calm and the air is still, I close my eyes and I am sure I hear the flutter of tiny wings. Is that a fairy, or maybe an angel, or was it perhaps a butterfly?

What little girl doesn't believe in or would not like to be a fairy or an angel? It seems a shame that we have to grow up if it means we have to give away such magical beliefs, don't you think? I believe that in being creative (my God-given gift) and by being in my garden, I am closer to God than at any other time – so why not have angels or fairies (call them what you will, as like the rose they are just as sweet) in my garden.

Fairies and angels are part of folklore around the world, from the romantic legends of medieval Europe, to stories known as the dreamtime that are passed on to young Aboriginal children in Australia from their Elders. Among the Aboriginal Dieri people it is believed that the whirls of dust which spring up suddenly in the bush (the Australian word for forest) were created by marching armies of fairies whom they called *Kutchi*.

Edward Knatchbull Hugessen (1829-93) wrote:

In the waning summer light
Which the hearts of mortals love,
'Tis the hour for elfin sprite,
Through the flow'ry mead to rove.'

Mortal eyes the spot may scan,
Yet our forms they ne'er descry,
Though so near the haunts of man
Merrily our trade we ply.
Ever mid the fragrant flowers,
With the songster birds and bees,
Practise we our magic powers
Loving playmates such as these.

From Charlie Among the Elves

Who cannot imagine this scene in their very own *Secret Garden*? I certainly can!

Sharman's Vintage Garden has so much love, family and friendship stitched into every embroidery and sewn into every seam, and I'm sure that if you look very closely and use your imagination, you will see fairies and angels in our *Sharman's Vintage Garden* quilt.

The following excerpt from Shakespeare's *The Merry Wives of Windsor* could easily have been (or perhaps is) stitched in with the spring flowers in *Sharman's Vintage Garden* quilt.

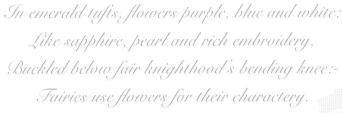

In emerald tufts, flowers purple, blue and white;
Like sapphire, pearl and rich embroidery,
Buckled below fair knighthood's bending knee:-
Fairies use flowers for their charactery.

Let your imagination run free, release your creativity and throw your fears away, as you enter the magical world of machine-embroidered quilting with Sharman's Vintage Garden *guilt.*

From the
GARDEN TOOL SHED

Essential tools, products and technology to ensure Sharman's Vintage Garden flourishes.

13

Sharman's
Vintage Garden
Quilt

And in green underwood and cover,
blossom by blossom the spring begins.
Algernon Charles Swinburne

Now open the gate to Sharman's Vintage Garden
to explore this enchanting machine-embroidered quilt,
with Jenny and Simon as your tour guides.

Seeds for
Sharman's
VINTAGE
GARDEN

NOTE: **Should you choose to 'fussy-cut' your fabric as we did, fabric requirements will differ according to the fabric pattern repeat.**

FINISHED SIZE OF QUILT: 98in (248.5cm) SQUARE

* Embroidery/sewing machine and accessories (either a 350mm x 360mm or 225mm x140mm (or larger) embroidery hoop)
* Design software and transfer device
* *Sharman's Vintage Garden* design CD (FREE with this book)
* Fabric:
  – 5yd x 45in (4.5m x 115cm) pale cream homespun for blocks, center medallion and cornerstones
  – 4yd x 45in (3.7m x 115cm) lime green lattice fabric for sashing, narrow borders and appliqué
  – 5–6yd (4.5–6.5m x 115cm) x 45in purple, pink and lime green vertical floral fabric for center medallion, quilt borders and small sashing cornerstones
  – 2yd x 45in (2.25m x 115cm) purple tone-on-tone fabric for narrow center medallion borders and binding
  – 118in (300cm) square quilt backing fabric (allowing 10in (25cm) on each side for long-arm quilting)
  – 2yd x 45in (2.25m x 115cm) cream nylon organza for optional *Embroidered Decoupage* appliqué hearts
* Three, 5yd x 60in (4.5m x 152cm) bolts of *Quilt Magic* lightweight fusible batting
* *Sheer Magic* to back fabric for embroidery and appliqué
* *Template Magic* printable sheets to print templates for multi-hooping of designs (this is not required if using the larger hoop)

* *Hoop Magic* self-adhesive tearaway stabilizer for embroidery
* *Cutaway Magic* for optional *Embroidered Decoupage* hearts
* Jenny's Japanese rayon 40 commercial threads: *purples*: three reels Gypsy Wind No 179, two reels Mulberry No 224, two reels Purple Jewel No 58, two reels Pansy No 59; *pink*: one reel Cherished Pink No 671; *greens*: one reel Celery No 82, one reel Paradise Hill No 174, one reel Band of Gold No 191, one reel Penny Hill No 231; and *gold*: one reel Medium Metallic gold No G3
* Jenny's *Invisa* sheer thread
* Construction thread for the needle and bobbin
* Pre-wound bobbins
* Machine feet: embroidery, open-toe, 1/4in patchwork/quilting with guide
* Microtex 80 needle
* Rotary cutter, self-healing cutting mat, quilting ruler
* Cutting shears
* Small sharp scissors
* Paper scissors
* Water-soluble fabric-marking pen
* Glass-headed pins
* 15in, 14 1/2in, 14in, 8 1/2in and 6in quilting squares or template plastic to make these
* Jenny's *Magic Stencil Wand* (optional)
* Spray bottle and water
* General sewing requirements

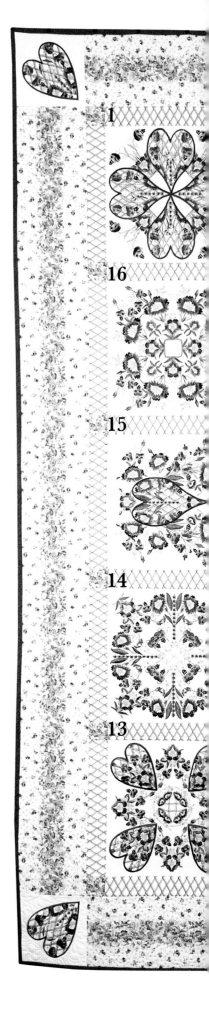

2

3

4

5

6

7

8

9

10

11

12

Center Medallion

Tilling the soil *in preparation*

IMPORTANT NOTE: Take the time to read and thoroughly understand the directions for Sharman's Vintage Garden quilt. Print the 'readme' file and the embroidery graphics (for your hoop size) for each block and become familiar with both before going any further.

THE THREAD color numbers (for *Sharman's Vintage Garden*) and sequence (using Jenny's glorious rayon embroidery threads) and thread stops are printed along with each graphic of the embroidery design to make stitching easy.

At all times, compare your actual quilt sections with those given in the instructions. Embroidering, piecing and quilting are not 'exact sciences', and although we have endeavored to be accurate with our measurements, yours may, at times, differ from ours. If this occurs, adjust your measurements to accommodate the differences.

Below you will find the instructions for all the fabric cutting, but we suggest you cut on a need-to-use basis. The embroidered quilt blocks, cornerstones and center medallion blocks will be cut to piecing size when the quilt is pieced.

CUTTING
REMEMBER: **Measure three times and cut once.**

JENNY'S TIPS
– **Find yourself a block of time in which you will not be interrupted, and choose an area that is both flat and well lit.**
– **Use a shot-of-steam iron to press fusible products to the back of the fabric, as the bonding agent is activated by both steam and heat.**

– **When you are bonding products to fabric, they should appear as one fabric with no wrinkles or puckering.**
– **Iron the *Sheer Magic* to the back of the soft cream homespun before cutting the 18in squares for the embroidered blocks.**
– **Cut out the fabric and *Quilt Magic* according to the instructions, and then iron the *Quilt Magic* to the back of the fabric, again making sure the fabric and batting appear as one fabric.**

1 Iron the *Sheer Magic* to the back of the pale cream homespun fabric, making sure you have no puckering or wrinkles and that the two appear as one fabric. *Sheer Magic* adds 'body'/thread count to fabric without altering the feel of it. This product is perfect for fine, sheer and open-weave fabrics such as silk chiffon, dupione and lightweight cottons that are to be embroidered. Iron the *Quilt Magic* to the back of the pale cream homespun over the *Sheer Magic*.

2 Use the rotary cutter, self-healing cutting mat and quilting ruler to cut firstly from:
Pale cream homespun fabric (backed with *Sheer Magic*) and *Quilt Magic*:
– 20, 18in squares for the embroidered quilt blocks and center medallion
– four, 8in squares for the center medallion border embroidered cornerstones
– four, 10in squares for the border embroidered cornerstones.

NOTE: **The sashing, borders and small cornerstones have been 'fussy-cut' in our *Sharman's Vintage Garden*. This is optional and takes extra time and fabric but the results are really worth it.**

'Fussy-cutting' means to cut fabric in such a way that the same fabric design element is cut for such quilt sections as the sashing, small floral cornerstones and the borders of the center medallion and quilt. This takes more time and fabric (the amount depending on the pattern repeat and the accuracy of the design printed on the fabric). You will need to 'fussy-cut' the fabric according to the printed design rather than the fabric grain. It has been our experience that most prints on fabric are not true vertically or horizontally, or with the grain of the fabric. This is especially true of vertical and horizontal pattern prints such as the floral fabric used for the borders and the lattice sashing strips.

The following quilt pieces should be cut on a need-to-use basis when you are piecing the quilt:
Lime green lattice fabric and *Quilt Magic*:
– 48, $2^1/2$in x $14^1/2$in for the sashing, block and center medallion borders
– four, $2^1/2$in x $31^1/2$in center medallion border strips.
The balance of the lattice fabric is used as appliqué fabric inserts for the embroidered hearts. It should have *Sheer Magic* ironed to the back of it.

Purple, pink and lime green vertical floral fabric and *Quilt Magic*:
– four, 6in x $35^1/2$in strips for the center medallion borders
– four, $8^1/2$in x $82^1/2$in strips for the quilt borders
– 36, $2^1/2$in squares for the block borders and center medallion cornerstones.

Purple tone-on-tone fabric and *Quilt Magic*:
– four, $1^1/2$in x $29^1/2$in strips for the center medallion narrow borders
– four, $1^1/2$in squares for the border cornerstones.

Purple tone-on-tone fabric only
– $3^1/4$in bias strips joined together on the bias to measure 11yd for the binding.

MARKING THE BLOCKS
3 Use the template plastic (or a medium-weight cardboard) to make accurate 15in, 14in, $14^1/2$in, 6in and $8^1/2$in squares with vertical and horizontal lines that intersect at the center marked on them.

(If you can purchase quilting squares of this size then do so.) These plastic squares will be used to mark the seamline on the 18in homespun squares and when cutting the embroidered blocks, center medallion and cornerstones to piecing size.
4 Use the quilting ruler or 14in square and fabric-marking pen to mark on the 20, 18in squares of homespun, vertical, horizontal and diagonal lines that intersect at the center, as well as a 14in centered square. These lines will be used for embroidery positioning and to ensure the embroidery field does not extend past the seamlines on the 16 quilt and four center medallion blocks.

5 Also mark the cornerstones (8in and 10in homespun squares) with vertical and horizontal lines that intersect at the center of the squares.

USING *TEMPLATE MAGIC* FOR MULTI-HOOPING
NOTE: If you have a hoop size that is larger than 225mm x 140mm but smaller than 350mm x 360mm you may choose to combine the designs for each block to suit your hoop size and thus minimize your number of hoopings per block. You may also be able to split the large designs. Please contact your software 'help' desk

if you are having problems splitting the large $13^1/2$in square embroidery designs.
6 If you are using the multi-hooping embroidery technique, you will need to use the *Template Magic* printable sheets to print the designs for each block on a need-to-use basis. *Template Magic* is a self-adhesive transparent 'paper', backed with a pressure-sensitive adhesive and covered with a protective backing. The designs are printed on the *Template Magic* side of the product (not the protective backing side). Use paper scissors to roughly cut out each design. (*Hint*: Keep the protective backing and back the templates with it after use so that they can be used again.)

7 The marked divide lines on the 18in homespun squares are used as guides for the placement of the printed templates.
8 We will use Block 1 as an example.

9 Position the four floral embroidery designs printed on the *Template Magic* of the diagonal marked lines, one in each corner, on the 18in homespun fabric square. Make sure all templates sit within the marked 14in square.

10 Position the four heart templates centered over the vertical and horizontal lines so the points of the hearts just meet in the center of the 18in homespun square.

11 Use the vertical and horizontal divide lines on the printed templates to mark corresponding positions on the 18in homespun square, and then use the ruler to connect these points. These intersecting lines now mark the placement position for each embroidery design that corresponds with the marks on the hoop.

12 Always embroider the designs in layers – starting with the bottom designs and working to the top. This way you can always overlap designs. For example, embroider the corner floral embroidery designs before the four hearts. Also, always embroider designs diagonal to each other rather than in a circular direction. By doing this, any slight variation from the true embroidery placements can be compensated for.

EMBROIDERY

NOTE: All embroidery designs on *Sharman's Vintage Garden* FREE design CD are color-sorted, using Jenny's correct thread colors (name and number) listed in embroidery sequence for each design. Make sure each design graphic is printed before you start embroidering each design or combination block design.

Using *Hoop Magic* self-adhesive tear-away stabilizer

13 The embroidery uses *Hoop Magic* self-adhesive tearaway stabilizer as a backing. This is hooped (regardless of the size of your hoop) and then the fabric to be embroidered is placed over the stabilizer rather than the fabric being hooped for the embroidery.

14 Hoop the stabilizer (with the protective coating uppermost in the hoop) and then use a pin to score the protective coating around the edge of the inside hoop and then diagonally in both directions, so the lines pierce the protective coating but not the stabilizer itself. Starting from the center of the hoop, remove the protective coating (four triangle segments).

15 Select your embroidery design on the machine so that it is centered on the screen with the needle in the center of the design. Place the fabric to be embroidered centered over the stabilizer in the hoop under the needle so the needle sits directly over the top of the intersecting marked placement lines. These lines should now correspond with similar marked positions on the hoop.

16 Use the basting/set stitch option on the machine to sew a row of stitching around the embroidery field on the fabric and secure the fabric to the stabilizer.

17 *Hoop Magic* is simply the best, as the adhesive is secure enough to hold the fabric to the stabilizer but easy to remove once the embroidery is complete. Also, it will not distort your stitching, the pile or the fabric when it is removed. Should you find you are getting a slight residue on your needle, however, remove it with a silicon wipe or Australian eucalyptus oil.

18 For those who are lucky enough to have a machine with a hoop that is capable of embroidering a design 13$\frac{1}{2}$in square, all that is left for you to do is embroider one block at a time in one hooping – this is so exciting! For those who don't yet have one, are you tempted to purchase one of these amazing new machines now?!

19 Use small sharp scissors to clip all the jump threads from the front and back of the embroidery. Also remove as much stabilizer as you can from the back of the embroidery. As *Hoop Magic* is made from plant and polyester fiber, if you dampen it (to make sure your fabric is color-safe), the stabilizer will pull away easily. If you choose to wash your embroidery, the stabilizer will disintegrate in the wash. How perfect is that!

20 The appliqué hearts used throughout *Sharman's Vintage Garden* and our accompanying projects use the embroidered appliqué technique. Turn to page 69 for step-by-step instructions on how to use this technique. Remember to iron the *Sheer Magic* to the back of the fabric to be embroidered. You may also choose to iron *Quilt Magic* to the back of the *Sheer Magic* to give added definition to the appliqué hearts.

21 Some may find it easier to apply the appliqué hearts to the embroidered blocks using *Jenny's Embroidered Appliqué Decoupage* technique, which is an alternative method.

22 Simply hoop *Cutaway Magic* and the cream nylon organza in the hoop and then stitch the embroidered appliqué hearts out as you would normally, following the step-by-step instructions on page 69.

23 When the embroidery is complete, remove the embroidered organza and stabilizer from the hoop. Use either small sharp scissors or *Jenny's Magic Stencil Wand* to cut/burn the excess organza/ stabilizer from around the outside edge of the hearts. These stand-alone hearts can now be applied to your quilt blocks (or project) in the exact required position, and then stitched in place around the outside edge using *Invisa* sheer thread and a small pin-stitch. For more detailed information about the many uses of *Jenny's Embroidered Decoupage* technique, see *Jenny's Heritage* book – the whole quilt is made using this technique!

THREADS

24 Jenny's glorious Japanese rayon 40 commercial threads are used throughout *Sharman's Vintage Garden*, giving the embroidery its lustrous finish. I prefer rayon threads as rayon is a natural fiber and has a slight stretch, which means that when the thread relaxes it fills in the embroidery completely. As these threads are industrial they are designed to be used vertically on a multi-spool holder. However, should you prefer to use them horizontally there is an adapter that you can obtain from RNK Distributing (email Debbie Homer at debbi@rnkdistributing.com).

Now it's time to plant your seeds – there are 16 garden beds to plant, along with the center garden plot. Enjoy watching your garden come to life as each quilt block begins to bloom .

25 Using fine pre-wound bobbins reduces the bulk of your embroidery and thus any chance of puckering. Use pre-wound bobbins that best suit your machine.

SOFTWARE

26 All the designs needed to complete all the projects in *Sharman's Vintage Garden* can be found on the FREE CD that comes with this book. This includes single designs for the smaller hoops (minimum size 225mm x 140mm) as well as the new large hoops. The combination large designs fit in a 350mm x 360mm hoop (13^1/2in square embroidery field). Remember for hoops in between these sizes you may choose to combine designs to minimize the number of hoopings required for each quilt block.

NOTE: We have endeavored to cover all formats for the embroidery designs, HOWEVER with technology moving ahead in leaps and bounds it is almost impossible to keep up with the constant changes in all brands of design software. If you have any queries in reference to your brand of software or combining designs in your software, please refer these to your software support team or local dealer.

If you do not have a software program, why not try Walter Floriani's embroidery software, with Walt giving you an onscreen tutorial and offering a wonderful help line. The 'help' desk for Walter's software is amazing.

27 Download the embroidery designs from the CD to the machine on a need-to-use basis for each quilt block or project; this way you will avoid confusion when you are stitching out the quilt blocks.

MACHINE

28 Ensure your machine is running smoothly before you start on a project this size. Have it serviced and clean the lint out of the bobbin area regularly, change the needle, and oil your machine according to your manufacturer's instructions. Many manufacturers suggest that there is no need to oil your machines which, in my experience, is correct, however I believe that when you are running a machine for long periods of time at a stretch, a few drops of oil in the bobbin area is advantageous. (Be sure, if you do this, to run the machine on a scrap of fabric to remove the excess oil before you start your project, to avoid getting oil on your precious work.)

Sharman's Vintage Garden quilt now awaits you – remember, from little things big things are made!

Embroidery designs used in

Block 1

svgbk01

*Single embroidery design for Block 1 using a 350mm x 360mm square hoop;
the block can be embroidered in one hooping.*

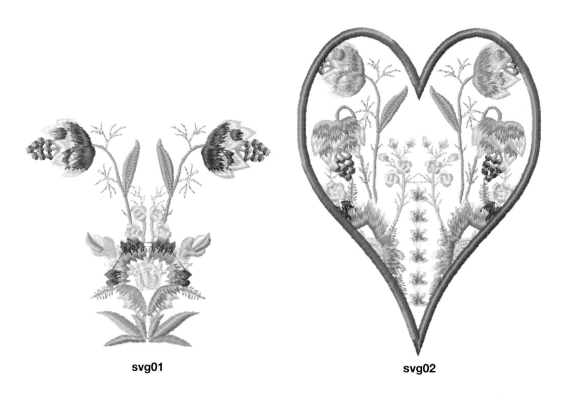

svg01

svg02

Individual embroidery designs for Block 1 using a 225mm x 140mm hoop.
The designs are listed in embroidery sequence.

Block 2

svgbk02

*Single embroidery design for Block 2 using a 350mm x 360mm square hoop;
the block can be embroidered in one hooping.*

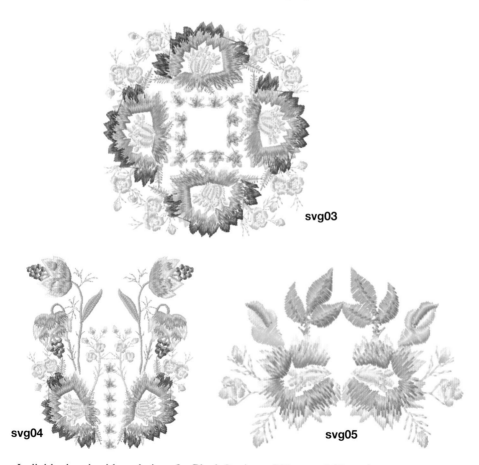

svg03

svg04

svg05

Individual embroidery designs for Block 2 using a 225mm x 140mm hoop.
The designs are listed in embroidery sequence.

Block 3

svgbk03

*Single embroidery design for Block 3 using a 350mm x 360mm square hoop;
the block can be embroidered in one hooping.*

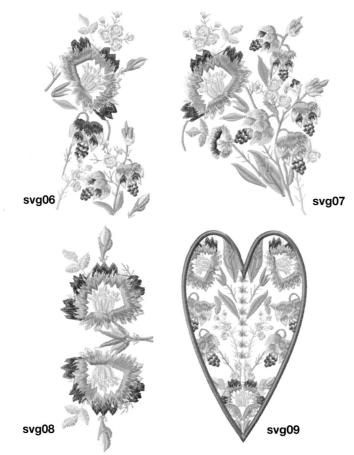

svg06

svg07

svg08

svg09

Individual embroidery designs for Block 3 using a 225mm x 140mm hoop.
The designs are listed in embroidery sequence.

Embroidery designs used in

Block 4

svgbk04

*Single embroidery design for Block 4 using a 350mm x 360mm square hoop;
the block can be embroidered in one hooping.*

svg10

svg11

Individual embroidery designs for Block 4 using a 225mm x 140mm hoop.
The designs are listed in embroidery sequence.

YOU ARE NOW *a quarter* OF THE WAY
THROUGH PLANTING YOUR GARDEN BEDS.

Block 5

svgbk05

*Single embroidery design for Block 5 using a 350mm x 360mm square hoop;
the block can be embroidered in one hooping.*

svg12

svg10

svg13

Individual embroidery designs for Block 5 using a 225mm x 140mm hoop.
The designs are listed in embroidery sequence.

Block 6

svgbk06

*Single embroidery design for Block 6 using a 350mm x 360mm square hoop;
the block can be embroidered in one hooping.*

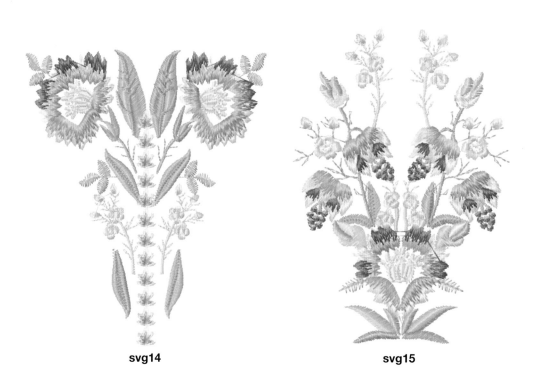

svg14

svg15

Individual embroidery designs for Block 6 using a 225mm x 140mm hoop.
The designs are listed in embroidery sequence.

Embroidery designs used in
Block 7

svgbk07

Single embroidery design for Block 7 using a 350mm x 360mm square hoop; the block can be embroidered in one hooping.

svg16

svg17

svg18

svg38

Individual embroidery designs for Block 7 using a 225mm x 140mm hoop. The designs are listed in embroidery sequence.

Block 8

svgbk08

*Single embroidery design for Block 8 using a 350mm x 360mm square hoop;
the block can be embroidered in one hooping.*

svg20

svg21

svg22

Individual embroidery designs for Block 8 using a 225mm x 140mm hoop.
The designs are listed in embroidery sequence.

HALF *The garden beds* HAVE NOW BEEN
PLANTED, AND HOW BEAUTIFUL THEY LOOK.

Block 9

svgbk09

Single embroidery design for Block 9 using a 350mm x 360mm square hoop; the block can be embroidered in one hooping.

svg23

svg24

Individual embroidery designs for Block 9 using a 225mm x 140mm hoop.
The designs are listed in embroidery sequence.

Embroidery designs used in

Block 10

svgbk10

*Single embroidery design for Block 10 using a 350mm x 360mm square hoop;
the block can be embroidered in one hooping.*

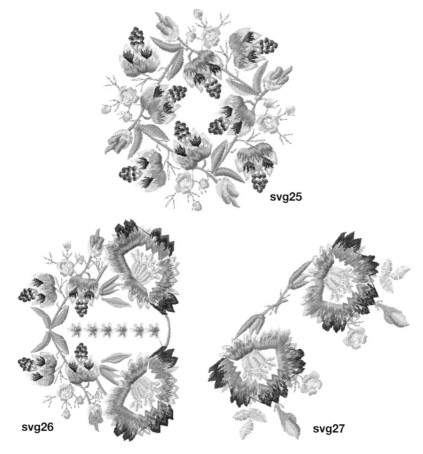

svg25

svg26

svg27

Individual embroidery designs for Block 10 using a 225mm x 140mm hoop.
The designs are listed in embroidery sequence.

Block 11

svgbk11

Single embroidery design for Block 11 using a 350mm x 360mm square hoop; the block can be embroidered in one hooping.

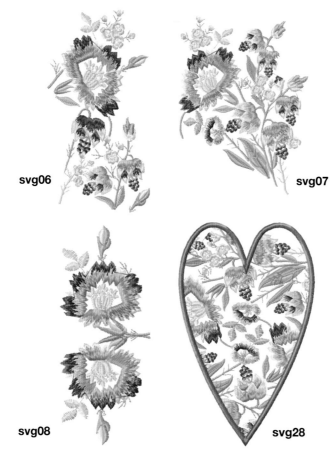

svg06

svg07

svg08

svg28

Individual embroidery designs for Block 11 using a 225mm x 140mm hoop. The designs are listed in embroidery sequence.

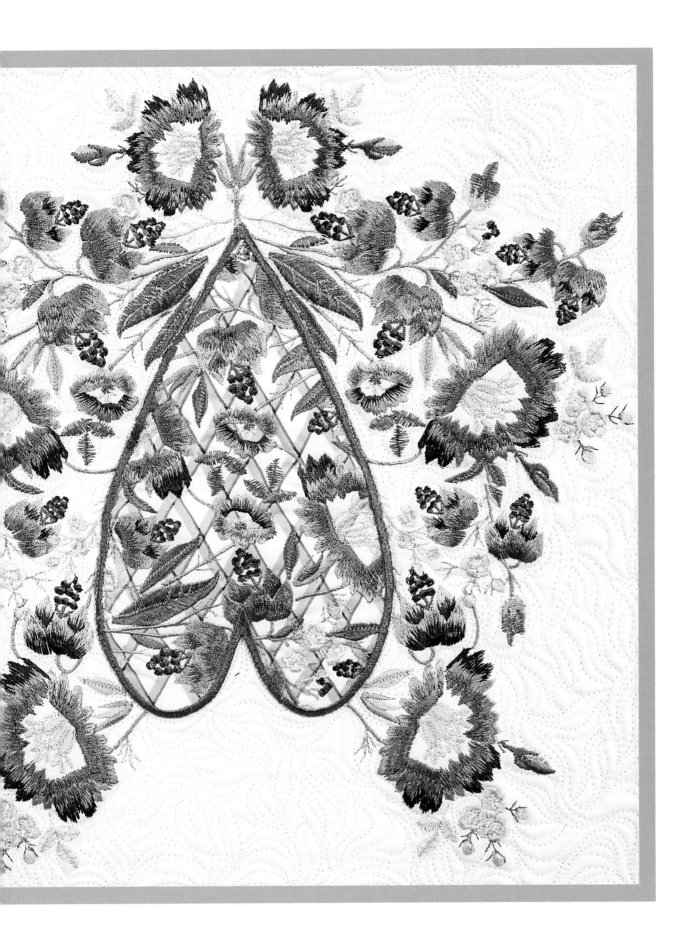

Block 12

svgbk12

Single embroidery design for Block 12 using a 350mm x 360mm square hoop; the block can be embroidered in one hooping.

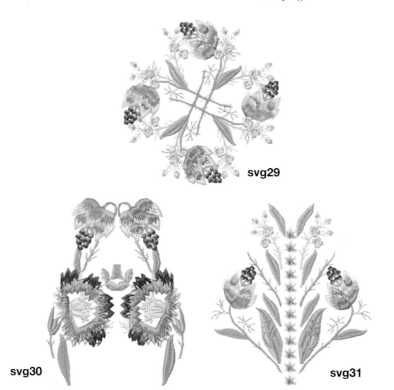

svg29

svg30

svg31

Individual embroidery designs for Block 12 using a 225mm x 140mm hoop. The designs are listed in embroidery sequence.

THE END IS IN SIGHT: ONLY FOUR MORE *garden beds* TO PLANT!

Embroidery designs used in
Block 13

svgbk13

Single embroidery design for Block 13 using a 350mm x 360mm square hoop; the block can be embroidered in one hooping.

svg32

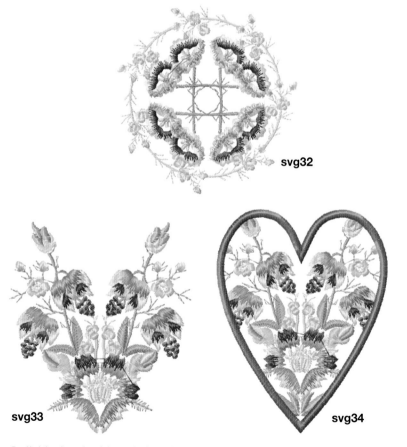

svg33

svg34

Individual embroidery designs for Block 13 using a 225mm x 140mm hoop.
The designs are listed in embroidery sequence.

Block 14

svgbk14

Single embroidery design for Block 14 using a 350mm x 360mm square hoop; the block can be embroidered in one hooping.

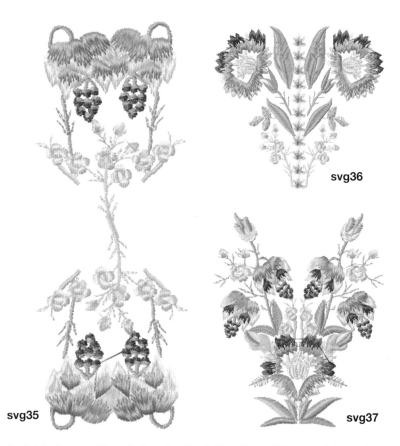

svg36

svg35

svg37

Individual embroidery designs for Block 14 using a 225mm x 140mm hoop.
The designs are listed in embroidery sequence.

49

Block 15

svgbk15

*Single embroidery design for Block 15 using a 350mm x 360mm square hoop;
the block can be embroidered in one hooping.*

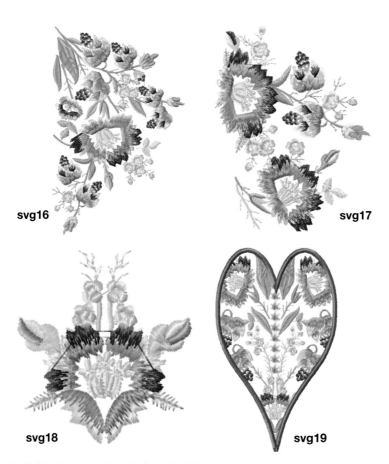

svg16

svg17

svg18

svg19

Individual embroidery designs for Block 15 using a 225mm x 140mm hoop.
The designs are listed in embroidery sequence.

Block 16

svgbk16

*Single embroidery design for Block 16 using a 350mm x 360mm square hoop;
the block can be embroidered in one hooping.*

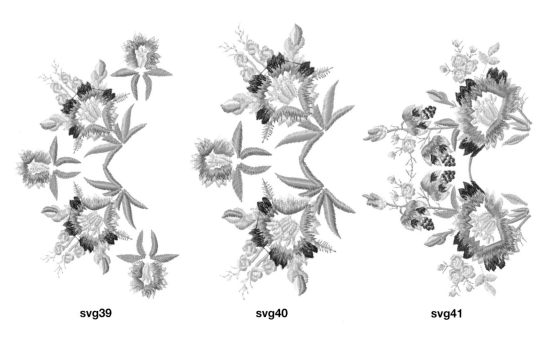

svg39   **svg40**   **svg41**

Individual embroidery designs for Block 16 using a 225mm x 140mm hoop.
The designs are listed in embroidery sequence.

YOUR *Sharman's Vintage Garden* BEDS ARE
NOW ALMOST ENTIRELY PLANTED – WATCH THE
GARDEN BLOOM AS THEY ALL COME TOGETHER.

Center Medallion
Embroidery

CONGRATULATIONS! YOUR *Sharman's Vintage Garden* BEDS ARE NOW ALL PLANTED AND READY TO BLOOM AS ONE, JUST AS SOON AS THEY HAVE BEEN COMBINED INTO THE ONE GLORIOUS GARDEN.

The center medallion is made up of four embroidered blocks pieced in such a way as to look like one embroidery.

Embroider two blocks the same of each center medallion single block design.

svgbkcm1   **svgbkcm2**

Single embroidery design for a center medallion block using a 350mm x 360mm square hoop; the block can be embroidered in one hooping. Embroider two blocks the same.

svg42   **svg43**   **svg44**

svg45   **svg46**   **svg47**

Individual embroidery designs for a center medallion block using a 225mm x 140mm hoop.
The designs are listed in embroidery sequence.
Embroider two blocks the same and two blocks that are mirrored horizontally.

The Garden Blooms
PUTTING IT TOGETHER

A QUILT should be put together when you have a period of uninterrupted time, and it should be laid out in an area that is large, flat, and has good light.

If you are using the 'fussy-cutting' technique you will need to ensure that each piece of fabric is marked with the direction of the top of the fabric (in a similar way to nap/shot silk). The top of the quilt and the top of the 'fussy-cut' fabric sections should be the same as each other.

When marking the wide center medallion and quilt borders, the fabric print can face in either a clockwise or an anticlockwise direction when pieced. When laying out the quilt in its entirety, it is important to have good light and be focused, and to label each quilt piece to ensure each section of the quilt faces in the correct direction.

NOTE: **Refer to the Layout Diagram on the opposite page and the photo of *Sharman's Vintage Garden* quilt on page 17 when you are cutting and piecing your quilt.**

EMBROIDERED CORNERSTONES

NOTE: **The center medallion borders and the quilt borders are joined together with embroidered cornerstones. Before you go any further, embroider these cornerstones using the lime green lattice fabric backed with *Sheer Magic* as the appliqué fabric inserts.**

1 For the center medallion border cornerstones, use the four, 8in squares of pale cream homespun to embroider design **svg34** (appliqué heart) centered on the diagonal.

2 For the quilt border cornerstones, use the four, 10in squares of homespun to embroider design **svg24** (appliqué heart) centered on the diagonal.

CUTTING TO PIECING SIZE

NOTE: **Do not remove the fabric-marking pen lines on the blocks at this stage as they will be used when piecing the quilt.**

Remember: Measure three times and cut once – always checking your actual measurements against those given in this book. Center a quilter's square (or one cut from template plastic) over the embroidered squares (for blocks and cornerstones) and use a fabric-marking pen to mark around them before cutting to piecing size on the marked lines. Accurate cutting and $1/4$in seams when piecing will ensure a flat quilt.

Embroidered 18in square blocks and cornerstones

3 Use the fabric-marking pen to mark around the quilter's squares and then the rotary cutter and quilting ruler to cut to piecing size the:

– 16, 18in square quilt blocks using a $14^1/2$in square
– four, 18in square center medallion blocks using a 15in square
– four, 8in square center medallion border cornerstones using a 6in square
– four, 10in square quilt border cornerstones using an $8^1/2$in square.

4 Refer to the photo of the quilt on page 17 as well as the block photos to mark the top of and number each quilt block and the cornerstones.

5 Refer to page 19 under the heading 'Cutting' to cut the sashing, wide and narrow borders and small floral quilt block border cornerstones. Place like pieces together, remembering to mark the top of the fabric (and the quilt top) and then label all the cut pieces.

6 Use a fabric-marking pen to mark the center of each sash and border strip.

LAYING OUT THE QUILT

7 Use a large flat area to lay out the quilt pieces, referring to the Layout Diagram and the photo of the quilt.

Master and his apprentice!

8 Lay quilt pieces out in the following order:

Center medallion:
– four, 15in center medallion blocks
– four, $1^1/2$in x $29^1/2$in purple borders and cornerstones
– four, $2^1/2$in x $31^1/2$in lattice borders and floral cornerstones
– four, 6in x $35^1/2$in floral fabric borders and embroidered cornerstones

Top and bottom block rows:
– three, $14^1/2$in blocks with two, $2^1/2$in x $14^1/2$in lattice sashing strips
– four, block borders made up of three, $2^1/2$in x $14^1/2$in lattice border strips connected with two, $2^1/2$in floral cornerstones

Side block rows:
– five, 14 1/2in blocks with four, $2^1/2$in x $14^1/2$in lattice sashing strips
– four, block borders made up of five, $2^1/2$in x $14^1/2$in lattice sashing strips connected with six, $2^1/2$in floral cornerstones

Borders:
– two, $8^1/2$in x $82^1/2$in floral top and bottom borders
– two, $8^1/2$in x $82^1/2$in floral side borders connect with two, $8^1/2$in embroidered cornerstones

PIECING

9 Use glass-headed pins to pin-quilt the pieces together prior to stitching. The pins should be horizontal to the cut fabric edge with the right sides of the fabric together, matching the center marked dots on the quilt pieces to those on the sashing and border strips. The ends of the sashing strips should match those of the blocks, and so on. Pin the pieces and then the sections of the quilt on a need-to-use basis.

10 Use the $1/4$in foot with a guide, and construction thread in the needle and bobbin, to piece the quilt and press all seams to the outside edge of the pieces/sections as you go.

Center medallion

11 Piece the center medallion in the following sequence to join:
– four, 15in embroidered center medallion blocks (ensure the embroidered hearts appear as one design, and press the seams open)
– two, $1^1/2$in x $29^1/2$in purple fabric strips to top and bottom
– four, $1^1/2$in square purple fabric cornerstones, one to each end of the two remain 29 1/2in strips, and then join these border strips to the sides
– two, $2^1/2$in x $31^1/2$in lattice strips to top and bottom
– four, 2 1/2in floral cornerstones one to each end of the remaining $31^1/2$in lattice strips and then join these to the sides
– two, 6in x $35^1/2$in floral fabric border strips to the top and bottom
– four, 6in embroidered cornerstones (hearts face outwards on the diagonal), one to each end of the two remaining $35^1/2$in strips and then join theses borders to the sides

Joining the blocks into rows

12 Join the $14^1/2$in blocks into rows with the $2^1/2$in x $14^1/2$in lattice strips in the following sequence:
– two, $2^1/2$in x $14^1/2$in lattice strips to Blocks 2–4, starting and finishing with a block (top row)
– two, $2^1/2$in x $14^1/2$in lattice strips to Blocks 10–12, starting and finishing with a block (bottom row)
– six, $2^1/2$in x $14^1/2$in lattice strips to Blocks 5–9, starting and finishing with a sashing strip (right side row)
– six, $2^1/2$in x $14^1/2$in lattice strips to Blocks 13–16 and Block 1, starting and finishing with a sashing strip (left side row).

Sharman's Vintage Garden quilt layout
Finished size of quilt: 98in (248.5cm) square

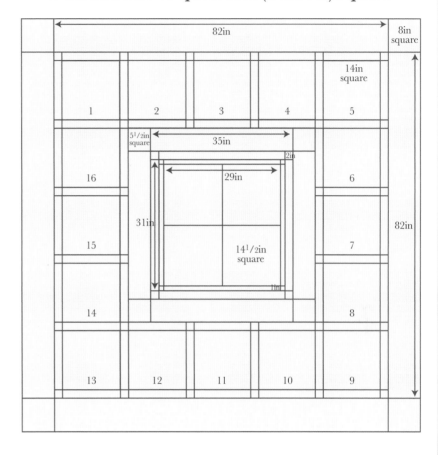

Joining the borders to the block rows

13 Join the $2^1/2$in x $14^1/2$in lattice strips with the $2^1/2$in floral fabric cornerstones in the following sequence:
– four, top and bottom block row border strips made up of three, $2^1/2$in x $14^1/2$in lattice strips pieced together with two, $2^1/2$in floral cornerstones, starting and finishing with a lattice strip. Join one border strip to each side of the top and bottom block rows
– four, side block row border strips made up of five, $2^1/2$in x $14^1/2$in lattice strips pieced together with six, $2^1/2$in floral cornerstones, starting and finishing with a cornerstone. Join one border strip to each side of the side block rows.

Putting it together

14 Join the bordered top and bottom block rows and the bordered side block rows to the center medallion.

15 Join two, $8^1/2$in x $82^1/2$in floral fabric borders to the top and bottom of the quilt. Join the four, $8^1/2$in embroidered border cornerstones, one to each end of the remaining two, $82^1/2$in border strips. Join these to the sides of the quilt.

Quilting

NOTE: **Remove all water-soluble pen marks using a spray bottle.**

16 Use the 118in square of fabric to back the quilt. You can either quilt *Sharman's Vintage Garden* quilt yourself or give it to a professional quilter as we did. Lizzy Allen worked her quilting magic on our *Sharman's Vintage Garden* quilt using *McTavishing* around the embroidery and continuous designs for the borders. (You can contact Lizzy via email at pallen30@bordernet.com.au to enquire about her amazing custom quilting.) Thank you Lizzy – you certainly added a touch of magic to *Sharman's Vintage Garden*!

17 Sign and date your quilt, then bind it in your preferred method using the $3^1/4$in x 11yd purple tone-on-tone bias fabric strip.

*Sharman's Vintage Garden is a constant
reminder of friends who, like spring flowers
(especially those in my favorite color purple),
seem to enfold me with their perfume of love and
beautiful support, just like a sumptuous quilt.
I couldn't agree more with the line from the movie
The Color Purple, that God would be displeased
with anyone who did not appreciate the color purple!*

**Sit back in awe of your *Sharman's Vintage Garden* quilt,
reflecting with the poet Keats when he wrote:**

*A thing of beauty is a joy for ever;
Its loveliness increases;
It will never pass into nothingness ...'*

Sharman's Vintage Garden

A
Cloister
of
Pillows

*Follow our magical
little butterfly as it flits
from pillow to pillow,
exploring the smaller
beds in our garden and
gleaning secrets of the
head gardener.*

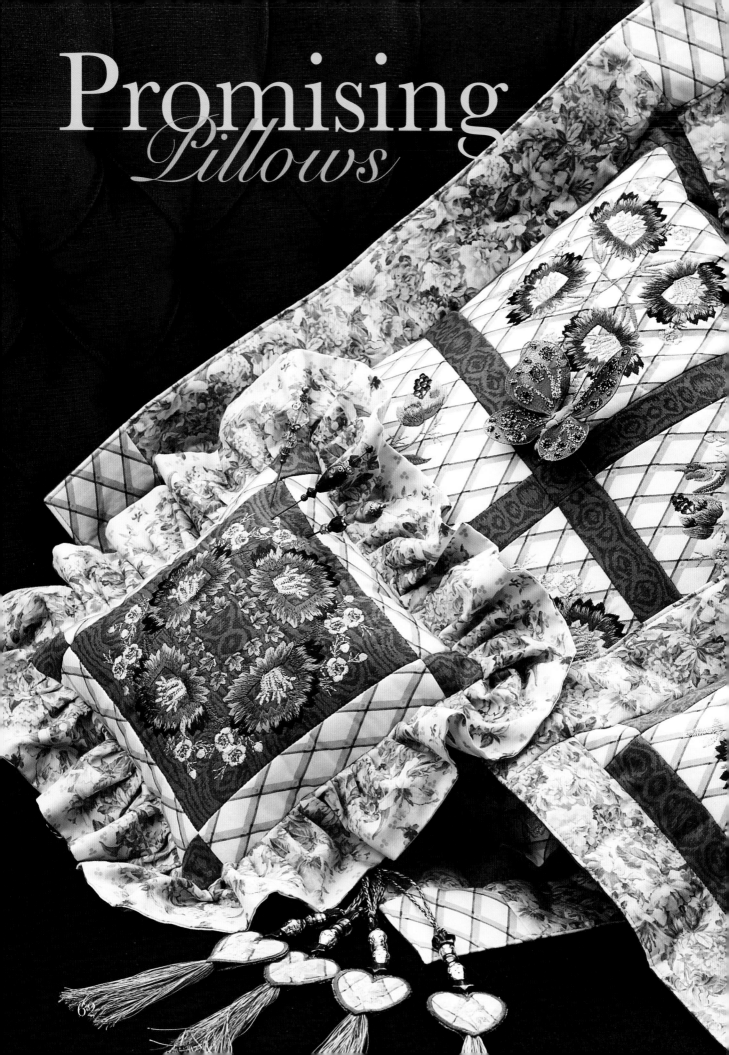

Promising
Pillows

There is no such thing
as too many pillows,
whether they're on a bed,
a couch or a garden swing.
Pillows are inviting and
romantic, and they blossom
along with Sharman's
Vintage Garden. What's
more, they're a great way
to use up the leftover fabric
from your quilt, especially
if you 'fussy-cut' as we did.

63

These clever and promising little pillows epitomize a favorite adage of mine: 'Just because something looks beautiful does not mean it has to be hard to craft.'

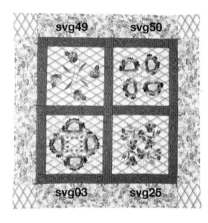

SIMON SEEMED to feel really left out of *Jenny's Heritage* (which of course he wasn't, as I cannot do without him), and so he was yearning to be creative and to show you just how easy it is to achieve beautiful things. What better way to do this than with these sumptuous yet easy to achieve delightful pillows.

Making pillows is cost effective (especially if you use fabric left over from your *Sharman's Vintage Garden* quilt or your fabric stash), and really straightforward as there are no rules – you can simply be creative! That's right – we give you permission to do whatever you like, so set your imagination free!

As with everything, color can make or break an item, so we suggest you choose your fabric and then match Jenny's rayon embroidery threads exactly with the colors in your fabric. Remember – less is best, and if in doubt leave it out!

The instructions to make these types of pillows can be found in most issues

HANDMADE EMBROIDERED PILLOWS BESTOW A PERSONAL TOUCH TO ANY BED; TUMBLED TOGETHER THEY INVITE YOU TO SINK BACK WITH A BOOK AND A SIGH AS YOU ESCAPE TO YOUR PERSONAL SANCTUARY.

of *Creative Expressions* and also in *Jenny's Heritage* book, which has 16 different ways to make pillows including the techniques we used in these three lovely little pillows. Refer to these sources if you need any help with construction. As for size, that is totally up to you.

Simply embroider the designs centered on, say, 10in squares of fabric backed with *Sheer Magic* and *Quilt Magic*, then cut the embroidered squares to your chosen piecing size. You might like to make larger pillows out of four of these squares which have been sashed and bordered with coordinating fabrics and then add a contrasting flange. (Our four block pillow used designs **svg03, 25, 49** and **50**.)

You could also use just one square to make petite pillows, and then add borders to the embroidered square, finishing it off with a flange or a folded ruffle. Our ruffle pillow used design **svg03** and our flange pillow used design **svg50**.

Petite pillows piled one atop another reminds me of a champagne fountain made with sparkling champagne glasses. They intrigue, invite, and look simply delicious. On top of a weathered garden bench, brightly colored pillows bring color and life to an otherwise aging retreat.

65

Weaving
A Dream Pillow

*Fabric can be made from
anything – you can even
create your own with ribbons,
braids and laces using Jenny's
Dissolve Magic Sticky.
This 'ribbon magic' weaving
technique is such fun, and the
results speak for themselves!*

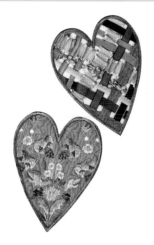

Ribbon Magic
WEAVING TECHNIQUE

This pillow is made up of four 7¹/2in square (finished size) purple fabric blocks (backed with Quilt Magic*) surrounded by a 'piped' ruffle. Two of the squares use the 'ribbon magic' weaving as an appliqué fabric insert in a heart, and the other two use it as the fabric upon which an embroidered appliqué heart has been stitched.*

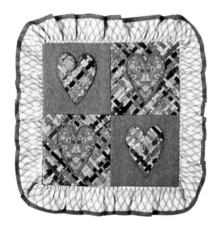

RUFFLE

1 The 'piped' pillow ruffle technique is achieved by seaming two contrasting fabric strips (lime green lattice for the front of the ruffle, and plain purple for the back of the ruffle and the 'piping'). The purple backing and 'piping' ruffle strip is ³/4in wider than the lime green lattice front ruffle. *Rule of thumb*: the length of the fabric for a ruffle is double the length of the pillow's circumference. The finished width of our ruffle is 3in.

2 Use a ¹/4in seam allowance to stitch the fabric strips together, and then join the two short ends together to form a circle. From the wrong side of the fabric, press the ruffle seam to the 'piping' fabric side. Fold the seamed ruffle strip in half width-wise (wrong sides of fabric together) so that the raw fabric edges are aligned, and then press the ruffle. Use your preferred method to gather up your ruffle so that it fits the outside edge of your pillow.

RIBBON MAGIC
WEAVING TECHNIQUE

3 *Dissolve Magic Sticky* is a fiber-based soluble stabilizer with an adhesive coating on one side which is covered with a protective backing.

4 Cut two pieces of *Dissolve Magic Sticky* that are each 1in wider than the size of the woven ribbon fabric you require. Use a pin to score (through the protective backing only) 1in in from the cut edges of the *Dissolve Magic Sticky*. Carefully remove the protective backing from inside the score lines.

5 You can use a selection of ribbons, braids, laces, yarns or cords for this technique. The secret is the wonderfully subtle combination of color and texture.

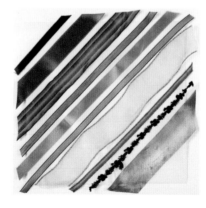

6 Decide whether you want straight or diagonal weaving and gently lay the selected ribbons, braids, etc, over the *Dissolve Magic Sticky* in one direction only.

7 By lifting up and then folding back every second ribbon or braid you have laid over the *Dissolve Magic Sticky*, you can then lay another ribbon or braid over the flat ribbons (and *Dissolve Magic Sticky*) in the opposite direction, and then replace the folded ribbons over the newly laid ones. For the second row of weaving, lift up and then fold back the ribbons that were left flat for the first row, and lay a second ribbon or braid over the flat ribbons, then fold the ribbons back over the newly laid

ribbon or braid. Repeat this process for the entire center area of your *Dissolve Magic Sticky*, remembering to leave only small gaps between the weaving rows.

8 Remove the entire protective backing from the second piece of *Dissolve Magic Sticky*, and place it flat over the woven ribbons, sandwiching them between the two layers. (If you have any creases in your *Dissolve Magic Sticky*, don't worry – this is a soluble stabilizer and will be washed out once the embroidery is complete.)

Embroidered Appliqué

9 Use *Hoop Magic* as the embroidery stabilizer hooped in the hoop to stitch the heart appliqué design **svg48** outline on the purple fabric square backed with *Quilt Magic*. (Overlock around the edges of the fabric and batting to hold them together and prevent fraying.)

10 Use pale cream homespun fabric backed with *Quilt Magic* as the first fabric appliqué insert in the heart outline.

11 Stitch the heart outline again and then use small sharp scissors to carefully cut around the outside edge of the heart close to the row of stitching.

12 Center the square of woven ribbons sandwiched between the two layers of *Dissolve Magic Sticky* over the padded appliqué heart.

13 Stitch the heart outline again over the woven ribbon, and then cut around it.

14 Complete the appliqué with a row of satin stitching around the outside edge of the heart. Make two.

15 Wash the *Dissolve Magic Sticky* soluble stabilizer out of the ribbon weaving fabric using warm water with laundry detergent and softener in it, swishing the fabric

around regularly. When the stabilizer and sticky have completely gone from the ribbons, and the *Hoop Magic* has been removed from inside the heart, rinse the block in clean water and lay it flat to dry.

16 Place a woven ribbon 'sandwich' over a fabric square backed with *Quilt Magic* and overlock around the edges of the layered fabrics to hold them together and prevent fraying. Use this as the base block for embroidered appliqué design **svg34**. Embroider the appliqué heart using the purple fabric backed with *Quilt Magic* as the appliqué insert fabric.

17 Use the thread colors used in *Sharman's Vintage Garden* and follow steps 9 to 11 for the appliqué fabric insert in the heart outline. Complete the embroidery and then repeat step 15. Make two.

18 Square up your four blocks and then join them together into a square. Stitch the 'piped' ruffle around the outside edge of the pillow top and then attach the pillow backing to the pillow in your preferred method. Turn the pillow to the right side, press it and then place an insert in your pillow.

See – a little 'ribbon magic' has happened right before your eyes! Believe in it and it will happen!

69

TITIVATING
Tassel Pillow

They hang on the end of cords, whether holding back divine drapes or at the end of a vintage bell-pull, or they can simply be used as a key or scissors minder. Tassels can be made of cords, ribbons, beads or, in this case, glorious threads. When attached to a pillow with petite embroidered hearts, these tassels add a unique finishing touch – the pillow you once described as simply 'pretty' is now nothing short of scrumptious!

Tassel Magic Pillow

Tassels are attention grabbers no matter where they are or what they are attached to! Tassels are intriguing; they have color and movement, and they captivate the eye. But trying to match tassel colors to fabric or trims can be time consuming, so I set about making my own – the results are here for all to see. We just love them, and Jenny's Magic Tassel and Fringe Maker *seemed to be the perfect name for this little tool.*

Making the pillow

1 Use a plain purple fabric square backed with *Quilt Magic* and embroider a heart (design **svg24**) vertically in the center of it. Next use lime green lattice fabric backed with *Sheer Magic* for the fabric appliqué insert to be embroidered in the heart.

2 The purple embroidered center square is bordered with the purple, pink and lime green vertical floral fabric, with purple fabric for the connecting cornerstones.

3 The feature of this pillow is the heart tassels that border it. You will need to embroider 16 hearts (design **svg63** using Jenny's *Embroidered Decoupage* technique (page 69). Use the *Cutaway Magic* hooped

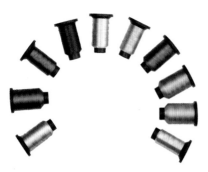

with cream nylon organza. Embroider the hearts and then use *Jenny's Magic Stencil Wand* or small scissors to carefully burn/cut around each heart.

Making the tassels

4 To make the tassels you will need:
– Jenny's rayon commercial threads in the *Sharman's Vintage Garden* color palette. Place the spools on the floor, knot all the threads together and then wind these threads all together on to the *Magic Tassel Maker*
– Jenny's *Magic Tassel Maker* tool
– needle and bobbin thread to match the tassel threads/cords
– large beading foot to suit your sewing machine
– machine needle.

5 Catch the threads in the slit at one end of the *Magic Tassel Maker* or, if they are too thick to go through this slit, hold them in place with a piece of sticky tape. Wind the threads vertically around Jenny's *Magic Tassel Maker* until you have the desired thickness (around 30–40 winds if you are using all the threads). Remember that the wound thickness of the threads will be doubled when you complete the tassel, and needs to be able to go through the beading foot. Again, catch the end of the wrapped threads through the slit or use sticky tape to hold them in place and prevent them from unraveling. (The length will be trimmed later.)

6 This technique uses a wide beading foot that is suitable for your sewing machine, thread that matches the tassel thread in the needle and bobbin, a wide zigzag (we use 7–9mm) with a length of 0.00mm, and the feed dogs lowered (as for free-motion stitching).

7 While the threads are still wound around the *Magic Tassel Maker*, slide them under and through the channel in the beading foot.

Now slowly slide the *Magic Tassel Maker* backwards and forwards under the foot until you have completely covered and wrapped the centre inch of the wound threads.

Remember to tie off at the beginning and end of the stitching to prevent it from unraveling.

8 Cut each end of the threads that are wound around the *Magic Tassel Maker* to free them.

Fold the tassel in half so that the two wrapped ends of the threads are aligned.

9 Pass a 'holding' cord through the folded tassel. This cord is then used to help pull

and guide the folded tassel through the beading foot in order for the stitching to hold the folded section of the tassel together.

10 Slide the folded tassel under and through the channel in the beading foot and repeat step 3 over the two wrapped ends of the tassel for no more than $1/4$in.

11 Trim the ends of the tassel to your required length. You now have a beautiful tassel in the color you want. A ribbon or cord may be threaded through the loop and then turned back on itself for around $1/2$in, and the end of the ribbon can then be wrapped (to cover the raw edges of the ribbon and secure it in place) in a similar manner to the tassel.

12 Make 16 tassels in this way.

13 Center a tassel in and to the back of each heart and use a washable fabric glue to secure it. Glue the hearts around the outside edge of the pillow once it is completed.

Making the twisted cord

You may also choose to make some additional beaded heart tassels to be used as key or scissors minders, or simply to look decorative. You will need three 6mm beads with a 3mm opening, two embroidered hearts and a length of twisted cord for each tassel.

14 To make a twisted cord by machine, you will need to measure out eight 1yd lengths of thread (again these can be combined). Knot both ends of the cords to hold them together. (You could also use normal embroidery thread but, as it is so much finer, you would need around three times the length to compensate.) You will also need an empty bobbin that is suitable for your machine.

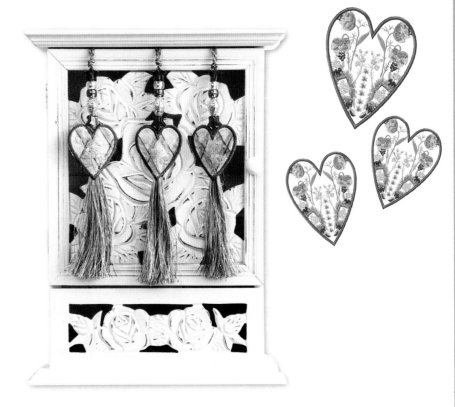

15 At one end of the knotted cords for twisting, pass a 3in 'holding' cord (this should be a strong fine thread) through the center of the cords and then tie the loose ends together. Now pass the knotted end of the 'holding' cord through the center of an empty bobbin. Place the bobbin on the bobbin winding spindle. (In using a fine strong 'holding' cord to pass through the center of the bobbin you can make your twisted cord as thick as you wish, as only the fine 'holding' cord goes through the center of the bobbin to twist the cord.)

16 Engage the bobbin winder while holding the knotted ends of the cord extended to their full length in your right hand. The threads will start to twist. When you feel them beginning to pull in toward the machine, stop the bobbin (with your left hand) while holding the threads taut. Keeping the threads taut, find the center of the twisted cord and hold the cord at this point with your left hand while taking your right hand (still holding the end of the cords) back to the bobbin to free the other end of the twisted cord.

17 Release your left hand; the two twisted cords will now twist on each other. Hold the two knotted ends of the twisted cord securely in your hand and knot them all together at that end. Use your hands to smooth out any twists in the cord that do not lay flat. You may find it easier to work with two people when you are learning this technique and especially if you are working with longer lengths of cords. These twisted cords are great to couch over or attach a tassel to the end of; they can also be used on garments as belt and button loops.

Putting the key/scissors minders together

18 Fold the twisted cord in half and then thread the folded end through the thread beads. Push the beads up the two cords, then loop the cord through the looped end of the tassel, bring the knotted ends through the loop and pull it tight.

19 Center the tassel at the back of one embroidered heart. Push the beads up the twisted cords until they sit just above the heart and tie a knot above and below the beads to secure them in position. Center the tassel at the back of an embroidered heart so that the tassel falls from below the point of the heart and the cords with the beads sit just above the 'V' at the top of the heart. Glue it in place. Glue the second embroidered heart over the back of the first heart (the one with the tassel glued to it), exactly matching the hearts so that they appear as one, and then glue it in place. You may need to use pins to hold the two hearts together until the glue dries. Finally, remove the pins.

How beautiful are these petite heart tassels!

73

'Hedged'
GARDEN PILLOW

*This delightful little pillow could be
likened to a garden bed surrounded by an
ornamental hedge. The 'hedge' is actually
a stunning fringe trim made using Jenny's
Magic Tassel and Fringe Maker, with
yarns and trims that complement the
embroidery and fabric of this 'garden' pillow.*

Natty Tress
TRIMMED PILLOW

I am always being asked where I obtain my glorious trims, especially the ones we use to adorn our pillows. Well, there is no need for you to search any more – you can make your own using Jenny's natty little Magic Tassel and Fringe Maker. *That's right – now you can create your own designer trims using the amazing yarns, ribbons and cords that are available these days, and it is so inexpensive. I find that the best variety (especially when it comes to knitting yarns) is available during fall and winter, so stock up in your favorite textures and colors during the colder months.*

THIS PILLOW is made from a 9in (finished size) square of lime green lattice fabric backed with *Quilt Magic*, with an embroidered appliqué heart (design **svg24**) in the center. The embroidered heart uses purple fabric (backed with *Quilt Magic*) for the appliqué insert. The flange borders use the purple, pink and lime green vertical floral fabric joined with purple cornerstones.

MAKING THE DESIGNER FRINGE TRIM

1 Wrap the variegated lime green and purple ribbon yarns together horizontally around the open center section of the *Magic Tassel and Fringe Maker*. Secure the starting end of the yarns (the cut ends) with sticky tape to prevent them from unraveling.

2 Place a matching piece of ¼in ribbon over the wrapped yarns down the center or to one side of the opening in the center of the *Magic Tassel and Fringe Maker*.

3 Use a narrow zigzag stitch and an open-toe foot to sew down the center of the ribbon, attaching it to the wound yarns.

4 Use small sharp scissors to cut the wrapped yarns on both sides of the *Magic Tassel and Fringe Maker*.

5 Slide the freed-up 'fringe' to the back of the *Magic Tassel and Fringe Maker* and repeat steps 1 to 5 until your fringe is the length you want it. Use larger dressmaking shears to straighten both cut sides of the fringe if necessary.

6 The ribbon now goes to the back of the fringe which is attached to the pillow flange with a straight or zigzag stitch or fabric glue, so that the inside edge of the fringe is aligned with and parallel to the seamline of the flange and pillow center.

7 If you choose to attach the ribbon down the center of the wrapped yarns, the result is a more 'fluffy' fringe which can be attached down the center to an item and then fluffed up to cover the stitching.

8 These 'magic' fringe trims can also be glued to the bottom of a lampshade or attached to the top of a purse or carry bag. Think of the possibilities and let your imagination soar.

'Flowers ... have a mysterious and subtle influence upon the feeling, not unlike some strains of music.'

HENRY WARD BEECHER. *EYES AND EARS*

From Sharman's Linen Closet

The creative team at Sharman's have designed these luscious linens, towels and pillows using subtle shades of soft pinks with a touch of blue. By adding embroidery designs in delicate colors to linens and bath towels, as well as a coordinating bolster pillow, these otherwise ordinary bedroom accessories have been transformed into handmade heirlooms.

svg58   svg59   svg60

A Passel of Colors

The gang at Sharman's just love working with scrumptious colors and threads, and the results speak for themselves. Jenny's thread colors used in these projects are Granny Smith No 201, Secret Garden No 42, Creamy Custard No 1542, Pretty Petunia No 46, Azalea No 1020, Metallic Gold No G3 and Metallic Copper No G31. In addition, each project has used only one design – svg22.

THE LINEN, towels and bolster pillow featured on pages 78–79 are wonderful examples of what can be done with a single design (**sg22**) from *Sharman's Garden* design CD. This design is vertically and horizontally combined and renamed **svg58**, **59** and **60**.

The towel and pillowcase feature a continuous embroidered border made up of design **svg58** combined vertically. If you have a continuous hoop, do what

Petrina has done and combine your designs to take advantage of this feature.

The linen sheet and pillowcase have been embroidered on directly, using *Dissolve Magic* as the stabilizer (it washes out with the first wash). The towel has a continuous embroidered strip (design **svg58**) of matching colored fabric attached to it, with a decorative braid covering the raw fabric edges. The embroidery designs are edged with decorative stitching. This stitching edges the embroidery to emulate an elaborate embroidered insertion braid. The decorative stitching is sewn on the bottom edge of the sheet and on both sides of the embroidery for the towel. White thread, an open-toe foot and *Tear-away Magic* as the stabilizer at the back of the stitching ensure perfect results.

As this product is made up of plant and synthetic fiber, it is easily removed when dampened and it does not distort the stitching. It will also wash completely away when the linen is laundered.

The sheet and bolster feature another combination of design **sg22**. This new design is **svg59** combined for the 350mm x 360mm hoop, and stitched along the top of the sheet and the center fabric insert in the bolster pillow as a continuous design. If you do not have this sized hoop, you can achieve the same result by combining design **svg58** for the continual horizontal embroidery and inserting design **svg60** for the intersecting vertical embroidery.

See what a little bit of imagination and color can do to your everyday linen and towels!

80

*Spilling from a chest of drawers or festooned over a
vintage washstand and basin, these glorious floral
linens celebrate embroidery, color and design, and
have been stitched with love and friendship.*

COTTON CANDY

Once again, Petrina has used her infinite supply of creativity to craft a continuous design of interlocking floral circles connected by baby pink ribbon and threaded through embroidered buttonholes on these gorgeous linen-closet items.

USING HER design software, Petrina combined two delicate circular floral designs (from the *Sharman's Garden* design CD), overlapping them and then inserting two buttonholes in the center of each circle. This new double circle design is **svg57**. These were again embroidered over a soft pink fabric strip, using the continuous hoop option, so the designs always match exactly. If you do not have this option on your machine, use the *Template Magic* technique (on page 19) to achieve the same effect for perfect placement and an equally perfect continuous border design.

Threading the baby pink grosgrain ribbon through the buttonholes completes this collection of sweet cotton candy linens and towels.

Sharman's Sewing Centers are tucked away in the friendly Texan towns of Longview and Tyler. Eager customers and students openly attest to the virtues of the amazing team at Sharman's: Sharman and Richard Dorsey (Richard is the token male who manages to keep 'his' gaggle of women in the store happy and fed at all times), Petrina Cude and Angie Wylie.

The stores are bursting at the seams with creativity, love and happiness, which are in endless supply to all who enter their doors. Customers travel for miles to partake in the endless feast that adorns the sewing tables at Sharman's

Sewing Centers. The sumptuous feast not only includes sewing machines and accessories, fabrics, trims, threads and notions, but education, inspirational classes, warm service and loving care, along with a satisfying dessert of dedication to the needs of the customers at all times. Trust me – once you have experienced Sharman's you will never want to go anywhere else.

If you would like to feast at Shaman's sewing tables, email: sharmans@aol.com or visit their website: www.sharmanssewingcenter.com They will be happy to answer any questions on these projects or their classes.

Candy for the eyes! Resplendent in their combination of color and design, these cotton candy linen-closet treasures will turn those menial day-to-day activities and chores into true delights!

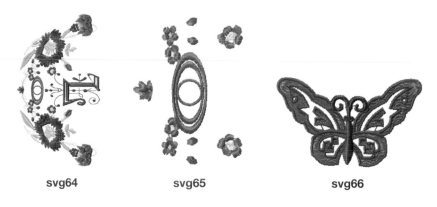

svg64   svg65   svg66

Flights of Fancy

Laura is an award-winning designer with a degree in Design and Textiles. She is an accomplished couture dressmaker, quilter, embroiderer and teacher, and one of the first and finest Accredited Jenny Haskins' Tutors (she was accredited in the year 2000). These days Laura is a valued team member of the RNK group who can be seen at all the major shows sharing her knowledge, expertise and abundant charm.

LEATHER is one of Laura's favorite materials to work with – she just loves embroidering on leather – and this stunning shoulder bag is perfect down to the last detail. It would easily pass as a designer accessory worth a small fortune, in fact I was only reading the other day of a celebrity who said she spent more on her handbag than she would on a small car! Laura uses the same quality materials and achieves the same look of famous designers but for a fraction of the price, and her purse is every bit the one-of-a-kind designer fashion item!

Laura used her software to combine designs from the *Sharman's Garden* design CD into a soft semicircle, inserting an oval (made up of two rows of satin stitching) with a circle in the center for the butterfly tassel closure (design **svg66**). She added her initial, the letter 'L' (from Jenny's *Antique Script and Frames* design CD), to the center of the design above the closure (design **svg64**). Laura also embroidered the purse flap lining using design **svg65** (matching the embroidered ovals for the closure to pass through).

The beautiful thread color combination used by Laura from Jenny's threads is:

Summer No 1173, Pine Green No 43 (for the leaves); Nutmeg No 620 (for the stems); Wine No 233, Dark Cranberry No 152, Dark Burgundy No 1008 (for the flower petals); Metallic Silver No G27 and Metallic Pink No G36 (for the flower centers). The embroidery is accented with ruby crystals, which make the embroidery glisten in a beautifully subtle way, as though the flowers have been kissed with early morning dew.

The beaded tasseled butterfly (design **svg66**) purse enhancer has been made using Jenny's *Magic Tassel and Fringe Maker* (see pages 72–73) using the three burgundy thread shades. Laura used soft pink silk backed with *Sheer Magic* as the appliqué fabric insert in the embroidered butterfly (taken from Jenny's *Butterflies for Catherine* design CD). The twisted beaded cord serves as the attachment and makes a delightful finishing touch. Having a handbag such as Laura's is like having a little of *Sharman's Vintage Garden* with you when you go out, right down to the butterfly – and you will be the envy of those celebrities! You can email Laura for the complete directions to make this *Flights of Fancy* purse at: laura@laurahaynie.com

Laura generously embroidered blocks for our *Sharman's Vintage Garden* quilt, including the center medallion, and she did so happily. Laura has been as exacting in every embroidered detail of the quilt as she is in her everyday life – so of course her embroidery is perfect.

Thank you Laura, not only for embroidering the blocks for us but more importantly for the many blessings you bring to Simon's and my life each and every day – you are like a little piece of heaven.

When Laura allowed texture and color to take a flight of fancy, the result was this fetching embroidered silver leather shoulder bag and beaded butterfly tassel purse enhancer.

85

Jenny's
ENDURING CLASSICAL SKIRT

*Laura and I have always flirted with full circular skirts, loving their feel,
look and drape, not to mention the romance of watching the circles flair out as
we twirl like leaves as they flutter down from a tree in the fall. I am always being
asked for the pattern of my* Enduring Classical Skirt *so, with a little help from my beautiful
friend Laura, here is the much sought-after pattern, which is oh-so-easy!*

ALTHOUGH MY SKIRT is 55-gore, Laura decided that a 50-gore skirt was perhaps a little more prudent for most figure types when she made hers. As the gores are joined onto a fitting stretch band of ribbing, those of you who have a fuller figure than Laura or I have, do not fear! This skirt does not add inches to your hips; rather it drapes beautifully and flatters any figure type.

MATERIALS
* ❋ Five, 1³/4yd x 45in (1.5m x 115cm) lengths of five coordinating fabrics: small, medium and large prints; plain; and tone-on-tone
* ❋ 2yd x 45in (1.8m x 115cm) length of your chosen fabric for the binding on the hem edge of the skirt
* ❋ 6in x 45in (15cm x 115cm) ribbing or Lycra for the skirt band
* ❋ 1in (2.5cm)-wide elastic for the band
* ❋ Serger/overlocker with threads that match your fabric for construction
* ❋ Rotary cutter (with a new blade), self-healing cutting mat and quilting ruler
* ❋ Pattern-making paper, lead pencil and ruler
* ❋ Paper scissors
* ❋ Fabric-marking pen
* ❋ General sewing requirements

ENDURING CLASSICAL SKIRT

PREPARATION

1 Use the pattern-making paper, lead pencil and ruler to make the skirt gore pattern. The gore is 1¹/2in wide at the top and extends to your desired length with a hem line width of 4¹/2in. Mark a vertical line that is the length you desire for your skirt. Measure out ³/4in on each side of the line at the top and then 2¹/4in at the hem edge and mark these points. Use the quilting ruler and the lead pencil to connect the marked points on each side of the center line, vertically and horizontally; this marks your personal skirt gore. Use paper scissors to cut the panel pattern out.

2 Press the five 1³/4yd x 45in lengths of fabric and then lie them flat, one on top of the other, over your cutting mat. Lay the panel pattern over the layered fabrics, then use the fabric-marking pen to mark around it. Flip the pattern to mark the second panel and then flip it again and again until you have 10 panels marked. Use the rotary cutter and quilting ruler to cut out the panels through all five layers of fabric.

3 From your chosen binding fabric, cut 3in strips joined on the bias to measure approximately 110in for the hem binding. Press it in half width-wise with the raw fabric edges aligned.

CONSTRUCTION

4 Use the serger/overlocker to construct the skirt panels. Arrange your fabrics in sequence and then piece your first five panels, then repeat the five panel sequence for the rest of the skirt.

5 Cut the 6in ribbing/Lycra to a length that fits comfortably around your hips. (It should be able to pass easily over your hips but still fit snugly around your waist.) Join it into a circle and then turn under a 1in casing on the waist edge.

6 Attach the waist edge of the skirt to the hip edge of the band of ribbing/Lycra, stretching the band as you go and slightly gathering the skirt if necessary.

7 Thread the 1in-wide elastic for the waist through the casing at the top of the band (again so it will stretch to pass easily over your hips but at the same time hold snugly to your waist).

8 Now try on the skirt and check its length, then mark up 10in from the hem edge of the skirt on the center panel of

the center five panels. Count seven panels out on each side of the marked panel and mark the edge of each one (this will encompass 15 panels). Mark and then cut a gentle curve that extends across the 15 front panels and also curves up to the marked 10in point.

9 Attach the 3in binding to the edge of the skirt, with the right sides of the binding and the skirt together and the raw fabric edges aligned and parallel, and then stitch from the wrong side of the binding. Leave a 6in binding tail and then attach the binding to the skirt hemline, stopping 6in from the start. Join your binding as you would for a quilt and then complete the stitching.

10 Press the overlocked seam of the binding toward the skirt and then top-stitch it in place around the bottom of the skirt panels, close to the binding seamline.

11 Wear your skirt with a long blouse or top (one that will cover the band at the top) and a jacket or vest of your choice, then enjoy the compliments and admiring glances of passers-by.

When I showed Laura my 55-gore Enduring Classical Skirt she fell in love with it, just as I had. In no time at all, our amazing Laura had a skirt of her own in fabric shades of soft pink and green, gentle colors that reflect her gentle loving ways.

I think of this skirt as a perfect standby – one that can be teamed up with a jacket (such as Laura's soft green ultra suede one). The center front of Laura's jacket features a lace-edged embroidered appliqué heart (design **svg09**), with fabric from Laura's skirt also used for the appliqué insert. The skirt can also be teamed up with a lace-edged strappy top for a more casual look, or a silk blouse for an after-five occasion.

I chose antique earthy shades for my skirt, with the fabric featuring divine fall roses. I teamed it up with a black top and patchwork vest that is encrusted with jeweled three-dimensional *Embroidered Decoupage* flowers. Robyn (who, by the way, is on a seven-week vacation in the Mediterranean as I write) chose shades of blue and white, her favorite colors, and wears it with a plain blue lace-edged top under an embellished jacket – it looks stunning.

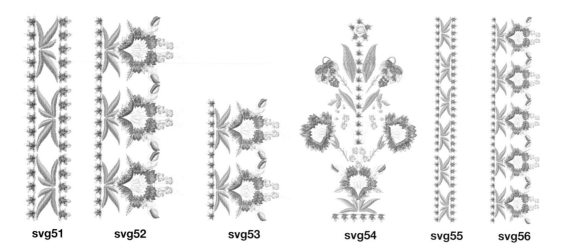

svg51 svg52 svg53 svg54 svg55 svg56

Enterprizing Women -
Times Two

I'm sure Regula and Bernadette must both have 'ingenious' as their middle names, as they develop products and services to the standard they want for themselves and then work hard to bring these concepts to the marketplace and their customers.

ALONG WITH THEIR KNOWLEDGE, wonderful customer service and friendship, these enterprising women are two of the most creatively driven people I have ever met in Australia. Their inspiring original class concepts, quilts and décor, as well as their dressmaking and tailoring innovations, are one of a kind and attract students from around the country as well as overseas.

Regula and Bernadette are almost an institution when it comes to feature artists in *Creative Expressions*, and they seem to outdo themselves each time, with every new item more creative than the last. This keeps their lives exciting – and ours!

Melann's Fabrics and Sewing Centre epitomizes their attitude to life, with the staff building into the business what they build into their lives – it is no wonder that the business is thriving.

Regula and Bernadette contributed to *Sharman's Vintage Garden* quilt by embroidering a number of the 13$\frac{1}{2}$in square combination embroidery block designs. When we asked them if they would do this, they agreed without hesitation. Thank you so much ladies; your talent and camaraderie are much valued virtues in Simon's life and my own.

SPRING GARDEN ESSENTIAL

Every lady's dream is to have an embroidered kimono like this one, which was created by the designing duo Regula and Bernadette from Melann's Fabrics and Sewing Centre in Adelaide, South Australia.

Taking a moment
TO DREAM

This kimono should not be restricted to the sanctum of the boudoir; try wearing it after a lavender bath at the end of a long day. Clip your hair up, pour your favorite drink and recline in your garden swing with your favorite CD playing softly in the background, harmonizing with the songs of the garden creatures.

Bernadette, our software expert, took designs from the *Sharman's Garden* design CD and simply played with them, cutting and pasting, and combining and deleting elements, to come up with the designs used on this kimono.

MATERIALS

❋ Embroidery machine and accessories (a continuous hoop would be an advantage)
❋ Design software
❋ Designs: **svg51** to **svg56** from *Sharman's Garden* design CD (FREE with this book)
❋ Burda pattern No 8134
❋ Soft green cotton Jacquard fabric for the kimono and silk lining according to pattern requirements
❋ Purchased soft pink narrow binding for the sleeves and front opening
❋ Jenny's rayon embroidery threads: Mint No 81, Celery No 82 (leaves); Wisteria No 220 (small flowers); Creamy Custard No 1542, Pink Posy No 3, Berry No 673 (main flowers and petite borders); White No 98 and Metallic Silver No G27 (flower centers)
❋ Machine feet: embroidery, zipper, construction
❋ Microtex 80 needle
❋ Fine pre-wound bobbins
❋ Construction thread
❋ *Hoop Magic* self-adhesive tearaway stabilizer
❋ *Template Magic* for embroidery placement
❋ Water-soluble fabric-marking pen
❋ Ruler
❋ Heavy-duty spray starch
❋ General sewing requirements

NOTE: The Burda pattern, fabric and Jenny's threads are all available from Melann's. Email them at melanns@bigpond.com – they are happy to ship.

PREPARATION

1 As with any fabric that is to be embroidered, you will need to allow extra for the front border panels, the sleeves and the pocket than the amount given on the pattern pieces.

2 Accurately cut out the kimono pattern pieces for the sleeves, pocket and front border panel and then roughly cut out the rest of the pattern pieces. Lay the pattern pieces over the fabric and trace around the cut-out pattern pieces using the water-soluble fabric-marking pen, leaving space around each piece. Roughly cut out the sleeve, front border panel and the pocket fabric pattern pieces and accurately cut out the other fabric pattern pieces.

3 Iron the pattern pieces to be embroidered using a heavy-duty spray starch.

4 Transfer embroidery designs **svg51** to **svg56** to the machine and print templates for the designs using *Template Magic*. See page 19 for directions on the *Template Magic* technique to ensure perfect placement.

EMBROIDERY

NOTE: Designs svg51 to svg53 suit a 140mm x 225mm hoop with designs svg54 to svg56 suiting a 360mm x 200mm hoop. Choose designs best suited to your hoop size.

Use the photo as guide to the thread colors and sequence used in each design.

5 All embroidery uses *Hoop Magic* in the hoop, Jenny's rayon embroidery threads as listed at the start of the project, a Microtex 80 needle, pre-wound bobbins and the embroidery foot. (Using *Hoop Magic* in the hoop eliminates the need for fabric hooping and makes embroidery placement easy; it also washes away easily when the fabric is first washed.)

Front panel

6 Embroider design **svg51** as a continuous border on the front panel border fabric pattern strip. If you have the option of using a continuous hoop, this is the perfect place for it.

Pocket and sleeve borders

7 Embroider design **svg53** across the top of the pocket and **svg52** around the sleeves as a continuous design.

Front of sleeves

8 Embroider design **svg54** centered on the front of each sleeve so it looks like an extension of the sleeve border design.

9 Remove excess stabilizer and clip all jump threads from the front and back of the embroidery. Iron the pattern pieces from the back and then replace the pattern pieces over the embroidered fabric. Re-mark the lines and then cut them out. Use clean water in a spray bottle to remove all fabric-marking pen marks/lines.

CONSTRUCTION

10 Construct the kimono following the pattern instructions and using the construction thread (in the needle and bobbin) and foot for the seams, and the zipper foot to insert the narrow piping down each side of the center embroidered front panel.

I can just see you, like me, wearing this wonderful kimono in your very own secret garden!

*The team from RNK Distributing was asked to
contribute a project to* Sharman's Vintage Garden *that
would show off Jenny's glorious rayon threads in
yet another optional color story.*

A Touch of Fall

A STUNNING CLASSICAL wrap is not only glamorous it is practical as well, being perfect to drape around your shoulders on a soft fall evening when visiting the opera or theater.

Sue Davis turned an everyday chocolate brown paisley pashmina has been transformed into a designer wrap that is reminiscent of the 1940s. Embroidery designs (from *Sharman's Garden* design CD: **svg68** (for a 360mm x 200mm hoop) and **svg62** and **svg67** (for a 140mm x 200mm hoop) have been stitched in harmonizing fall thread shades, with three combination designs being equally spaced along the length of the pashmina. The appliqué fabric inserts are in a soft cream silk, backed with *Sheer Magic*. The intriguing fringing and tassels were made using *Jenny's Magic Tassel and Fringe Maker*.

The thread colors used are Baby's Breath No 1156, Rosa No 188, Positively Pink No 1672 (large flowers); Acorn No 622, Milk Chocolate No 186 (stems, leaves and flower centers); Natural Flesh No 227 (small flowers); and Metallic Copper No G31 (flower centers).

You can email Debbie Homer: debbie@rnkdistributing.com for the instructions to make this fall wrap.

Glistening Midnight

Black silk serves as the canvas for yet another
thread color palette option for embroidering
Sharman's Vintage Garden.
The self-patterned silk fabric has been
fashioned into a lightweight wrap
with curved ends.

94

THE WRAP IS TAPERED at one end; the wider end slips through an opening in the narrow end to secure it, allowing the wrap to drape across the front of the body (with the filigree embroidered border of the wrap to the waist). The elaborate embroidery on the wider end is then passed over the shoulder. A generous sprinkle of heat-activated crystals completes this enchanting wrap, created by Sue Davis.

The designs used on the wide curved end of the wrap are: **svg25** for the center with **svg22** on each side of it. This design is extended with **svg61** which is a filigree feature along the waist edge of the wrap. The narrow end of the wrap is also curved and has a decorative beaded drop.

The thread colors used in *Glistening Midnight* are a perfect example of how a limited thread color palette in graduated shades of midnight blue can show off an embroidery. The thread colors Sue used are Blooming Flax No 603, Soft Serenity No 140, Caribbean No 64 (flowers); Trinket No 676 (stems and leaves); and Metallic Gold No G3 (flower centers).

Thank you Team RNK – these wraps are stunning and the thread color choices are simply scrumptious! You can email Debbie for the directions to make this silk wrap: debbie@rnkdistributing.com

Margaret's
Magenta Garden

Margaret loves working with vibrant thread and fabric colors that mirror her personality and energy. When she was in Australia to be trained as the first International Jenny Haskins' Accredited Tutor, Margaret was intrigued with the 'piped' prairie points which were on the Princess and the Pea pillow, taught at one of the classes. Her Magenta Garden quilt attests to Margaret's saying, "There is no such thing as too many 'piped' prairie points." There are a mere 96 of them in this quilt!

Margaret is a long-time and much valued friend of Simon's and mine, who just happens to also be a gifted tutor and an experienced and talented machine embroiderer. She is now a freelance teacher who travels the US sharing her knowledge and expertise with generosity and patience. As one student emailed me, 'Margaret is a wonderfully patient teacher who sends her students away with the self-confidence to take what is taught in class home and use it with the assurance that the results at home will emulate those in class. This is wonderful, however I must say the life skills she imparts to her students are as valuable as the techniques taught in class, as I use them in my day to day life.' This statement says it all about Margaret, who was also happy and willing to be part of our team and embroider several of the blocks in Sharman's Vintage Garden *quilt. Thank you Margaret for the love and support you give both Simon and me – it goes way beyond our professional relationship. You are the best.*

MATERIALS

❋ Embroidery/sewing machine with accessories (hoop 225mm x 140mm)
❋ Design software and transfer device
❋ *Sharman's Vintage Garden* design CD (FREE with this book)
❋ Fabrics:
– 2¹/₂yd x 45in (2.3m x 114cm) hot pink silk for 'piped' prairie points, borders, sashing and binding
– 1yd x 45in (91cm x 114cm) olive green silk to pin-tuck
– 2¹/₂yd x 45in (2.3m x 114cm) floral fabric for 'piped' prairie points and rectangular blocks
– 2¹/₂yd x 45in (2.3m x 114cm) cream fabric for embroidered blocks and backing fabric
❋ *Quilt Magic* lightweight fusible batting
❋ *Sheer Magic* to back the olive green silk and the cream fabric for the embroidery
❋ *Tearaway Magic* to back the decorative stitching on the 'piped' prairie points
❋ *Hoop Magic*, self-adhesive tear-away stabilizer
❋ Jenny's rayon embroidery threads: Citrus Cloud No 692, Cherry Soda No 1018, Azalea No 1020 (flowers); Perfect Olive No 1204 (two reels), Pine Green No 43 (leaves and stems); Ray of Light No 190 (centers); and Light Gold No G1 ('piped' prairie points and quilting)
❋ *Invisa* sheer thread for quilting
❋ Fine pre-wound bobbins
❋ Construction thread
❋ Machine feet: open-toe, embroidery, ¹/₄in quilting/patchwork, open-toe clearview freehand, quilting guide
❋ Machine needles: Microtex 80, 2mm twin
❋ Rotary cutter, self-healing cutting mat and quilting ruler
❋ Water-soluble fabric-marking pen
❋ Glass-headed pins
❋ Small sharp scissors
❋ Quilt basting spray
❋ General sewing requirements

Finished size of quilt: 50in (127cm) square

PREPARATION

1 Use the design software, transfer device and the *Sharman's Vintage Garden* design CD to transfer design **svg47**, **svg03** and **svg50** to the machine.
2 Use the rotary cutter, self-healing cutting mat and quilting ruler to cut from:

Hot pink silk:
– two, 3³/₄in x 43¹/₂in strips for top and bottom borders
– two, 3³/₄in x 50in strips for side borders
– four, 1¹/₂in x 10³/₄in strips for block sashing
– two, 1¹/₂in x 21in strips for top and bottom floral fabric block borders
– two, 1¹/₂in x 43¹/₂in strips for side block row border
– nine, 4¹/₂in x 45in strips for 'piped' prairie points
– 3¹/₂in bias strips joined together to measure 205in for quilt binding.

Cream fabric:
– eight, 12in squares for embroidery, backed with *Sheer Magic*
– 52in square for quilt backing.

Olive green silk:
– 1yd x 45in, backed with *Sheer Magic*, for twin-needle stitching.

Floral fabric:

– four, 10³/4in x 21in rectangles backed with *Sheer Magic* to connect the outside embroidered blocks.

3 Use the 2mm twin needle threaded with Perfect Olive thread, a pre-wound bobbin, the open-toe foot and a wave stitch to pin-tuck the olive green silk with a horizontal/vertical ¹/2in grid using the quilting guide.

4 Cut the pin-tucked olive green silk into 16, 6¹/4in squares and then cut these on the diagonal to make 34 triangles.

5 Use the fabric-marking pen and ruler to mark four of the 12in cream fabric blocks with vertical and horizontal lines that intersect at the center (for the corners). Mark the remaining four with diagonal lines that intersect at the center (for the center).

EMBROIDERY

6 All embroidery uses the embroidery foot, the Microtex 80 needle, embroidery threads from the materials list, pre-wound bobbins and *Hoop Magic* stabilizer in the hoop.

7 Embroider the heart design (**svg47**) centered on the diagonal on the four diagonally marked 12in cream fabric squares, omitting the appliqué fabric inserts in the design.

8 Embroider flower design **svg03** centered on the two vertically/horizontally marked 12in cream fabric squares, and flower design **svg 50** on the remaining two squares.

9 Remove the excess stabilizer from the back of the embroidery, clip the jump threads and then iron each square. Square up each of the eight squares to 8in.

'PIPED' PRAIRIE POINTS

10 Use the ¹/4in quilting/patchwork foot and construction thread in the needle and bobbin to join one 4¹/2in x 45in hot pink silk strip to a matching floral fabric strip, right sides together and stitching down the full 45in length.

11 From the wrong side of the fabric, press the ¹/4in seam allowances to the side of the hot pink silk fabric. On the right side of the fabric, you can now turn the hot pink fabric to the back of the floral fabric over the ¹/4in seam and press it flat. The raw fabric edges will not align – this is fine.

12 By folding the floral fabric back down over the hot pink silk fabric at right angles, the edge strip of the backing fabric can be seen and appears as a piped edge. Pin the folded fabric on each side and cut the long side parallel with the raw fabric edges of the folded fabric. Repeat the folding, pinning and cutting for the length of the pieced fabric strip.

13 Margaret chose to stitch a decorative oval satin stitch along the piped edge of the hot pink silk using Light Gold metallic thread, the open-toe foot, a pre-wound bobbin and *Tearaway Magic* at the back of the fabric.

14 With the pieced fabric strip open flat, embroider the decorative stitch along the hot pink silk so the stitch is aligned with and parallel to the seamline – the stitch should show on the 'piping' fabric. Remove the *Tearaway Magic* from the back of the stitching. Adding stitching to the 'piping' fabric gives it a decorative edge – a special touch for your 'piped' prairie points.

15 Again, fold the hot pink silk fabric strip to the back of the floral fabric strip over the 1/4in seam and then press it. Repeat step 12 to fold your fabric into a 'piped' prairie point. Join all nine 41/2in x 45in hot pink and floral fabric strips and then sew the decorative row of stitching along the seamline over the hot pink silk. Repeat step 12 until you have 96 'piped' prairie points.

16 The prairie points should measure 11/2in from the folded point to the raw fabric edge. Cut your 'piped' prairie points to this measurement.

ATTACHING THE 'PIPED' PRAIRIE POINTS

17 Pin three equally spaced 'piped' prairie points to each side of the eight 8in square embroidered blocks (12 per block),

with the wrong side (the floral fabric) of the 'piped' prairie points to the right side of the embroidered blocks. The raw fabric edges of the 'piped' prairie points and the block should align, and the points of the prairie points should point to the inside of the embroidered block. The angled sides of the corner prairie points should be aligned and just touching.

18 Stitch the 'piped' prairie points to the eight 8in blocks using the open-toe foot and construction thread close to the raw fabric edges.

PUTTING IT TOGETHER

19 Use the photo on page 99 and the layout diagram on page 101, construction thread in the needle and bobbin and the 1/4in quilting/patchwork foot to construct the quilt.

20 Mark the center of the long bias side of the 32 olive green silk pin-tucked triangles. Match the center of a triangle with the center of one side of the 8in embroidered square edged with 'piped' prairie points. With the right sides of the block and the triangle facing, stitch the triangle to the embroidered block. Use a hot steam iron to press the triangle back over the seam so that the seam faces the triangle fabric side. This now forms part of the block.

21 Working in a clockwise direction, pin and then stitch a second triangle to the next side of the block. Repeat the ironing as in step 20 and then repeat the stitching and pressing of the triangles for the four sides of the block.

22 On the right side of the fabric blocks, measure out 1/4in from the seamline where the olive green silk triangles

overlap, and mark this point on all four sides of the block. Use the quilting ruler and fabric-marking pen to draw lines through these points that are parallel with the seamlines, making a square on the block. Check that this marked square is 103/4in and then cut along the lines. Repeat for all eight blocks.

23 The four embroidered heart blocks are for the center, and the floral embroidered blocks alternate for the corners.

24 Piece the quilt in the following sequence, referring at all times to the layout diagram.

Center medallion

– join two, 103/4in center heart blocks so that the hearts face to the top right and left, row A
– join two, 103/4in center heart blocks so that the hearts face to the bottom right and left, row B
– join rows A and B together so that the upper curves of the hearts face to the four corners and their points face to the center
– join the 11/2in x 21in hot pink silk narrow border strip to the top and bottom of the center medallion
– join the 21in x 103/4in floral fabric rectangle to the top and bottom of the center medallion.

Side blocks

Join the four embroidered blocks, the two floral rectangles and the four 11/2in x 103/4in hot pink sashing strips into side block rows:
– join a 11/2in x 103/4in hot pink sashing strip to each 103/4in side of the 21in two floral rectangles

Magenta Garden quilt layout diagram
Finished size of quilt: 50in (127cm) square

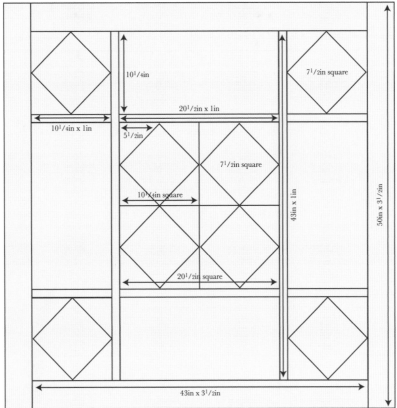

10¹/₄in

20¹/₂in x 1in

10¹/₄in x 1in

5¹/₂in

7¹/₂in square

7¹/₂in square

10¹/₄in square

43in x 1in

50in x 3¹/₂in

20¹/₂in square

43in x 3¹/₂in

– join a different embroidered 10³/₄in block to each side of the hot pink sashing strips (two side block rows)
– join a 1¹/₂in x 43¹/₂in narrow hot pink border strip to the inside edge of the two side block rows (make sure that there is a different embroidery design at the top of these rows so that the same embroidery designs will be diagonally opposite each other when the side block rows are attached)
– join a side block row to each side of the center medallion.

Borders
– join a 3¹/₂in x 43¹/₂in hot pink silk border strip to the top and bottom of the quilt

– join a 3¹/₂in x 50in hot pink silk border strip to each side of the quilt.

QUILTING
25 Press the quilt from the right side of the fabric and then iron a 50in square of *Quilt Magic* to the back of the quilt top.
26 Use the basting spray (following the manufacturer's instructions) to attach the 52in square of cream backing fabric to the back of the quilt.
27 Use thread (as directed) in the needle, a straight stitch, and thread that matches the backing fabric in the bobbin, to quilt using the following:
– the open-toe foot and *Invisa* sheer thread to stitch in-the-ditch in all the seamlines

– the open-toe clearview freehand foot and Light Gold metallic thread to free-motion quilt around the embroidery in each block, carefully lifting up the 'piped' prairie points so as not to catch them in the small stipple quilting design
– the open-toe clearview freehand foot and *Invisa* sheer thread to free-motion quilt the floral fabric rectangles using a large stipple quilting design.
28 Square the quilt sides up to 50in and then use the 3¹/₂in x 205in hot pink silk bias strip as the binding, attaching it in your preferred method for a ¹/₂in finished size.
29 Sign and date your *Magenta Garden* quilt, and smell the garden scent!

*This is such a wonderful project to complete our book with. Thank you Margaret –
as always you have the winning edge. You can contact Margaret via email at
Mzmoorehead@aol.com for information on her class schedule.*

Things that make *our garden grow ...*

KAY BROOKS

Creating the Jenny Haskins' Magic range of products has been extremely fulfilling for me and the entire RNK team. As any successful gardener knows, the fundamental foundation for prize-winning flowers and veggies is a rich, nutrient filled soil, and I like to compare the Magic range of stabilizers to this soil!

WE USE ONLY the best fibers and adhesives for each of our stabilizers in this range and have created a variety of styles to fit every fabric and embroidery need for all embroidery applications. I have listed below a brief description of each stabilizer for your convenience. Use it as a quick reference guide for your next sewing project.

Cutaway Magic lightweight fusible polyester stabilizer

This fusible stabilizer is a must for embroidery on delicate knits or stretch fabrics. Its sheerness will not shadow through light-colored garments and its fusible feature prevents shifting during the hooping or embroidery process. It is also a must when stitching 'freestanding' embroideries for Jenny's *Embroidered Decoupage* technique as there is no need to wash out the stabilizer from the embroidery. *Cutaway Magic* can literally be cut away or burnt away from around the edge of the embroidery using the Magic Stencil Wand, leaving soft stand-alone embroidery that can then be applied to any garment or quilt. *Cutaway Magic* comes in 12in or 20in x 10yd rolls.

Dissolve Magic Sticky water-soluble stabilizer

This stabilizer is used for delicate embroidery in hard-to-reach areas, or for fabrics that can be damaged by the hooping process. The sticky surface is ideal for holding items in place while you embellish them. Because *Dissolve Magic* rinses away (remember to use a water softener and liquid detergent to completely

remove the 'sticky' property, and then rinse it in clean water), it is perfect for projects that require the removal of all the stabilizer, such as christening gowns snd linens. *Dissolve Magic Sticky* comes in 12in or 20in x 10yd rolls.

Dissolve Magic fiber-based soluble stabilizer

Create elegant lace, freestanding embroideries or appliqués with this remarkably stable, fiber-based water-soluble product! This product is also ideal for stabilizing sheer delicate fabrics when there can be no trace of stabilizer left behind! *Dissolve Magic* fiber-based soluble stabilizer rinses clean and leaves your project beautiful and soft! It comes in 12in or 20in x 12yd rolls.

Heat Magic heat-dissolving stabilizer

This stabilizer is used to keep embroidery stitches elevated and uniform on the surface of high-pile and textured fabrics. Because *Heat Magic* is removed with the touch of an iron, it is ideal when embellishing or embroidering luxury fabrics such as velvet, silk and linen, or fabrics that cannot withstand water. *Heat Magic* is also ideal for decorative machine stitches such as those used for heirloom and appliqué techniques. *Heat Magic* comes in 10in or 20in x 10yd rolls.

Hoop Magic self-adhesive tear-away stabilizer

This stabilizer is used for embroidery in 'hard-to-hoop' areas such as collars and

cuffs, or bulky items such as towels, blankets and quilt blocks that have been backed with *Quilt Magic*. *Hoop Magic* self-adhesive tear-away stabilizer is a must when embroidering fabrics that can be damaged by hooping, such as velvet, corduroy or leather. It is a mixture of plant and synthetic fiber which has a light adhesive on one side to hold most items in place while they are being embellished; it then tears away easily from most stitch types. If necessary, *Hoop Magic* can also be easily removed from the back of embroidery without damaging the stitching, by simply dampening the stabilizer. *Hoop Magic* comes in 12in or 20in x 10yd rolls.

Quilt Magic lightweight fusible batting

This batting is a needle-punched, super light, fusible quilt batting/fleece that is soft and flexible, allowing you to create 'non-bulky' quilted garments that drape and move freely, as well as quilts and home décor items. The fusible feature of this amazing lofty fleece will help to eliminate puckering and will hold the fleece and fabric together through quilting, embroidering and laundering. *Quilt Magic* is 59in wide and comes in 1yd or 5yd bolts.

Sheer Magic delicate fabric backing

Delicate fabrics can be damaged by the embroidery process due to the constant needle penetration. *Sheer Magic* provides a solution by creating a protective barrier for the stitching to form in without changing the drape of the fabric. It also adds 'thread count', without bulk, to delicate fabrics such as silk, satin, dupioni, taffeta and silk or rayon velvet without altering the feel or drape of the fabric, and it prevents fabric fraying. This is not a stabilizer; it is a fabric support and should be used at the back of all delicate fabrics no matter what they are used for, be it embroidery, quilting, garment construction or appliqué. *Sheer Magic* ensures perfect results with no puckering every time, and it comes in 30in x 3yd packs.

Sheer Magic Plus open-weave support backing

Open-weave fabrics can be damaged and easily pucker due to the embroidery process. *Sheer Magic Plus* is used to add 'non-bulk' support when embroidering dense designs on such fabrics as quilt-weight cotton, batiste and linen, giving these fabrics a stabilizing boost without adding stiffness to the fabric or design. *Sheer Magic Plus* comes in 30in x 3yd packs.

Tearaway Magic eco-friendly tear-away stabilizer

This eco-friendly tear-away stabilizer makes an ideal backing for airy, open-work embroidery designs on light cottons and linen. It is easily removed from satin stitching and won't harm the delicate fibers of heirloom-quality fabrics as it can be dampened and then removed easily without damaging your stitching. It is also available in pre-cut sheets for printing foundation piecing designs for patchwork and quilting! *Tearaway Magic* comes in 12in or 20in x 10yd rolls, or 8^1/$_2$in x 11in 20-sheet packs.

Tearaway Magic Fusible is a fusible eco-friendly tear-away stabilizer

The light fusible coating of this eco-friendly tear-away will help prevent the fabric from stretching or distorting during the hooping and embroidery process. It is ideal for embroidery on quilt cotton, linen, shirt-weight denim, silk and more. It is also perfect for decorative stitching as it holds the fabric to the stabilizer while being stitched and can be re-heated to remove the stabilizer once the stitching is complete. It also prevents the fabric from puckering or being pulled up under satin

stitch-based decorative stitches. *Tearaway Magic* comes in 12in or 20in x 10yd rolls.

Template Magic pressure-sensitive printable template paper

Use this pressure-sensitive, printable product to create templates for your next embroidery project, and achieve perfect placement of your embroidery designs without stress! Print your embroidery design directly on *Template Magic*, which you can now 'stick' to the surface of your garment or quilt for a perfect guide for embroidery placement. Each template can be used many times by simply returning it to the protective backing paper after each use. *Template Magic* is a must for multi-design placement as it allows quick, easy and accurate placement when you want to visualize where a design would look best on a garment. *Template Magic* comes in 8^1/$_2$in x 11in 20-sheet packs.

Water-Soluble Magic soluble topping

This 'topping' is essential for keeping your stitching uniform and elevated on textured surfaces. Place this product over the surface of most fabric types and then embroider directly over it. When stitching over this product it allows the stitches to relax and align, leaving your embroidery smooth and even. *Water-Soluble Magic* rinses away completely and leaves no residue when your embroidery is finished. It comes in 10in or 20in x 10yd rolls.

Web Magic pressure-sensitive double-sided fusible web

This double-sided fusible web is perfect for fabric appliqué projects as it doesn't alter the feel of the fabric; instead it leaves it soft and flexible, making it perfect for your next quilt, home décor or garment project! The pressure-sensitive side allows for easy positioning or repositioning of appliqué fabric with accurate placement when you are working with intricate patterns. Enjoy the needle-friendliness of this product for flawless stitching, and use the printable sheets as a shortcut when you are doing embroidered appliqué in the hoop! Print the appliqué insert design on a *Web Magic* printable sheet, fuse this to the back of the fabric to be used for your appliqué

and then carefully cut it out. When the appliqué outline in an embroidery design is stitched, simply place the fabric cut-out backed with *Web Magic* over the outline and press it in place, then continue with the embroidery design – there is no need to remove the hoop from the machine any more for embroidered appliqué! *Web Magic* comes in 9in x 5yd rolls or 8^1/$_2$in x 11in 20-sheet packs.

The vigor or excellence of any garden can be judged by its color in foliage and flower, and so it is with embroidery! Jenny's luscious, high-sheen, Japan-made Rayon threads add a vibrant hue to any stitching. There is also a range of flawless metallic threads which stitch like a dream, even at high speeds. Our *Magic* range of thread will make your embroidery burst into life, just like a beautiful flower!

Embellishment is a word we use constantly when we work with Jenny's and Simon's concepts. They are masters of adornment, and having the correct tools is absolutely necessary. We are proud to announce the addition of the *Magic Stencil* and *Crystal Wands*. These tools are (again) made to very specific applications for perfect embossing. The *Magic Stencil Wand* (which heats to the perfect temperature) is used to create stunning freestanding embroidery to be used in Jenny's *Embroidered Decoupage* technique, and the *Magic Crystal Wand* is perfect for applying the *Magic* range of heat-activated crystals to add 'bling' to any foundation.

Fringes, tassels and beads are also essential ingredients for Jenny's techniques. The recently released *Magic Tassel and Fringe Making Tool* allows you to custom-make tassels and fringe-trim to match your fabric. The new *Magic Semi-Precious Bead Collection* and hand-picked silk dupioni packs will add the final touch to your assortment of must-have *Magic* products.

Ricky and I started the Haskins' line with only five products … my how this garden has grown! Our journey in this industry has been an amazing experience. Working alongside Jenny and Simon has been a deam-come-true for us and one of the best things to have ever happened for RNK Distributing. And the most exciting part of our association is knowing the best is yet to come!

A tribute to the 'constant gardeners'...

A garden is only as good as the gardeners who lovingly plan it, cultivate the soil, 'sew' the seeds, feed and water the plants and then sit back in wonder as they watch it all bloom. So it has been with our Sharman's Vintage Garden, *and our talented team of 'gardeners' who contributed so much to this book.*

A BEAUTIFUL architect-designed garden doesn't happen on its own – behind any venture we undertake there is always a team of (what often seems like) thousands, but in reality it is oh-so-few. Jenny and Simon would like to acknowledge their gifted 'gardeners', as they give credit to and thank this talented team who tended *Sharman's Vintage Garden* and helped make this book happen (once again) almost overnight.

Editor: Jenny Haskins

Quilt: From the studio of Jenny and Simon Haskins

Publisher: Thanks to *Simon Blackall* and *Diane Wallis*, the talented duo from *The Watermark Press* who have been with us from the start back in 1999, and who always know what to do when it comes to publishing and then do it with class. Thank you once again for your input, friendship and support in yet another book – *Sharman's Vintage Garden*. Simon, you certainly are our 'constant gardener'.

Publisher: *Ricky* and *Kay Brooks* from RNK Distributing. This is their second book for us, following on from the success of *Jenny's Heritage*. Ricky had already been planning a second book while *Jenny's*

Heritage was still in pre-production, and broke the news to Jenny in stages so she wouldn't panic! Ricky is always coming up with some kind of plan, and often he has it all worked out in his head before he even mentions it to anyone, leaving the unsuspecting person to find out only when it happens! "Ricky has Jenny doing things before she has even thought of them." I remember when I wrote that for *Jenny's Heritage*, mentioning *Sharman's Vintage Garden*, and here I am at the end of it, having taken the photos and written it in just a week. Ricky, oh great Sultan – can one of your harem (this one) have a holiday next?! But this is what makes Ricky and Kay so amazing; they just go from one success to the next, sweeping you along with them (even if it means carrying you at times)! They are the type of people who 'make things happen' rather than asking what has happened. Thank you also for supporting the *Jenny Haskins'* product line (which is growing like Jack's beanstalk), not to mention your friendship.

Designer: This is our second book with designer *Jo Martin*, and what a wonderful ongoing experience it is. Not only is she an amazingly talented designer, she is so accommodating, happy and professional. Nothing is a bother to Jo, and pages seem to be back to us before we have even sent them to her (well, it seems that way sometimes). Jo had the cover for *Sharman's Vintage Garden* designed and back to us in record time – she really gets into my head. Thank you Jo – you certainly are an amazing 'gardener'.

Subeditor: *Nina Paine* is able to take what I write and edit it in such a way that is clear and to the point, yet retains my (hopefully) warm and fuzzy 'voice', making it a pleasure to read. I cannot wait to get my text back from her and read it once again, this time with awe at the miracle she has performed with her magic editing – it makes me look much

better than I really am! Nina as always is very patient and understanding and so thorough when it comes to waging her way through my somewhat disjointed text! Thank you Nina, you are great at pulling out the weeds in my 'garden' of text.

Photographer: Tom Evangelidis, photographer extraordinaire! Tom captures the mood, color and style in every shot, thus making anything he photographs look better than the real thing. This time he took the photos in record time and he had to put up with me as the stylist, ably assisted by Simon. Simon responded warmly to our every wish and kept us well-fed and watered, with everything at our fingertips. This allowed Tom to work his magic with his camera, producing photographs with classic charm and style that reflect his amazing talent (it must stem from his Greek ancestry).

Stylist: *Robyn Wilson*. Robbie has been overseas, cruising the Mediterranean and Europe on a seven-week vacation while we produced this book. However she is always present in our hearts and lives, even when she is not here. Simon and I filled in for her while she was enjoying the warm Mediterranean sun. But I have just been reading what I wrote last time, in

Jenny's Heritage, and it was Simon who was on vacation then, so I think my turn must be coming up! As always, Robbie, your warmth, friendship and creative talent endear you to all who cross your path. You are part of this book in absentia.

Barbara, Al, Clifford and *Joshua Wallach*, of Halcraft, who are the not-so-new 'kids' on the block now as this is also the second book they have contributed to with Jenny and Simon. Combined they are a family business, one that is now an integral part of the *Jenny Haskins'* product line which, after all, is just like a garden – it grows every day, and is lovingly tended by Cliff who is indeed a gifted 'gardener'! It is a joy to have you all on our gardening team – you know exactly how to create an atmosphere in which gardens flourish and bloom in all seasons. Thank you for your support in everything we do – you are the best.

Maree Mulvaney, my long-time friend and one of the most stunning ladies I have ever known. Maree's beauty transcends age like an amazing flower that never wilts. Thank you for allowing us to use your glorious house (which reflects your style and grace) for the photography – it certainly was the perfect setting to showcase *Sharman's Vintage Garden*.

Our 'constant gardeners' make the world a better place; let's celebrate them!

JENNY HASKINS' DESIGN COLLECTION
Jenny's 'seed' catalog for when next planting your Secret Garden ...

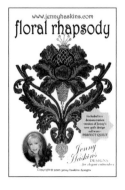

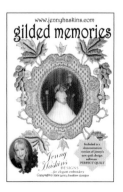

robyn's romance

rose buds

roses for mary

sharman's garden

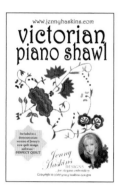

twin needle shadow work by machine

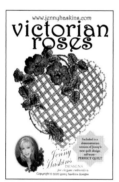

victorian bows & baskets

victorian embroidery the heart

victorian fantasy with fans

victorian pansies

victorian piano shawl

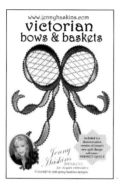

victorian roses

victorian script & antique frames

victorian scrolls & curlicues

vintage needlework

available from:

Unique Creative Opportunities (Australia)
Phone: 61 2 9680 1381
Fax: 61 2 9680 1381
Email: simon@jennyhaskins.com
www.jennyhaskins.com

RNK Distributing (US)
For all Jenny's products, including CDs, stabilizers, batting, threads, fabrics, beads, books and magazines, phone: toll free 1877 331 0034
Email: info@RNKDistributing.com

Remember, 'the more you share your love the more there is to share'. Share your love of machine embroidery and you will be amazed at where it will lead you. You have so many gardens other than Sharman's Vintage Garden to plant, so get busy planting your seeds. In the meantime, Jenny and Simon are busy planting their own artistic 'gardens' to bring joy to the creative eye and soul in every one of us.

Other Books/Magazines
By Jenny Haskins

Victorian Dreams	Sally Milner Publications
Color Purple	(sold out) see *Creative Expressions* No 12 & No 13 for directions
The Federation Quilt	(sold out) see *Creative Expressions* No 15 to send for directions on a similar quilt
Amadeus	Aussie Publishing
Inspirational Machine Embroidered Quilting (Arsenic and Old Lace quilt)	Aussie Publishing
Victorian Pansies	Quilter's Resource (sold out)
Victorian Roses	Quilter's Resource (sold out)
Victorian Splendor	Quilter's Resource (sold out)
Inspirational Home Décor	Brother Australia (sold out)
Latte Quilt with Kerrie Hay	Quilter's Resource
Roses for Mary	Quilter's Resource
MarJen for Error, *CE Special*	Pride Publishing (Creative Living Media)
Simon's Folly, *CE Special*	Pride Publishing (Creative Living Media)
Spectacular Fashion, *CE Special*	Pride Publishing (Creative Living Media)
Moulin Rouge, *CE Special*	Pride Publishing (Creative Living Media)
Fragrant Delights, *CE Special*	Creative Living Media
Creative Expressions Magazine	Creative Living Media
Aquamarine Ambience	Quilter's Resource
Summer Wine	Quilter's Resource
Jenny's Heritage	RNK Distributing
Sharman's Vintage Garden	RNK Distributing